Microsoft® Official Academic Course

Microsoft .NET Fundamentals
Exam 98-372

WILEY

VP & PUBLISHER	Don Fowley
EDITOR	Bryan Gambrel
DIRECTOR OF SALES	Mitchell Beaton
EXECUTIVE MARKETING MANAGER	Chris Ruel
MICROSOFT PRODUCT MANAGER	Anne Hamilton of Microsoft Learning
EDITORIAL PROGRAM ASSISTANT	Jennifer Lartz
ASSISTANT MARKETING MANAGER	Debbie Martin
SENIOR PRODUCTION MANAGER	Janis Soo
ASSOCIATE PRODUCTION MANAGER	Joel Balbin
CREATIVE DIRECTOR	Harry Nolan
COVER DESIGNER	Georgina Smith
TECHNOLOGY AND MEDIA	Tom Kulesa/Wendy Ashenberg

Cover photo: © Ralph Lee Hopkins/NG Image Collection

This book was set in Garamond by Aptara, Inc. and printed and bound by Bind-Rite Robbinsville.
The cover was printed by Bind-Rite Robbinsville.

www.wiley.com/college/microsoft *or*
call the MOAC Toll-Free Number: 1+(888) 764-7001 (U.S. & Canada only)

Foreword from the Publisher

Wiley's publishing vision for the Microsoft Official Academic Course series is to provide students and instructors with the skills and knowledge they need to use Microsoft technology effectively in all aspects of their personal and professional lives. Quality instruction is required to help both educators and students get the most from Microsoft's software tools and to become more productive. Thus our mission is to make our instructional programs trusted educational companions for life.

To accomplish this mission, Wiley and Microsoft have partnered to develop the highest quality educational programs for Information Workers, IT Professionals, and Developers. Materials created by this partnership carry the brand name "Microsoft Official Academic Course," assuring instructors and students alike that the content of these textbooks is fully endorsed by Microsoft, and that they provide the highest quality information and instruction on Microsoft products. The Microsoft Official Academic Course textbooks are "Official" in still one more way—they are the officially sanctioned courseware for Microsoft IT Academy members.

The Microsoft Official Academic Course series focuses on *workforce development*. These programs are aimed at those students seeking to enter the workforce, change jobs, or embark on new careers as information workers, IT professionals, and developers. Microsoft Official Academic Course programs address their needs by emphasizing authentic workplace scenarios with an abundance of projects, exercises, cases, and assessments.

The Microsoft Official Academic Courses are mapped to Microsoft's extensive research and job-task analysis, the same research and analysis used to create the Microsoft Technology Associate (MTA) and Microsoft Certified Information Technology Professional (MCITP) exams. The textbooks focus on real skills for real jobs. As students work through the projects and exercises in the textbooks they enhance their level of knowledge and their ability to apply the latest Microsoft technology to everyday tasks. These students also gain resume-building credentials that can assist them in finding a job, keeping their current job, or in furthering their education.

The concept of life-long learning is today an utmost necessity. Job roles, and even whole job categories, are changing so quickly that none of us can stay competitive and productive without continuously updating our skills and capabilities. The Microsoft Official Academic Course offerings, and their focus on Microsoft certification exam preparation, provide a means for people to acquire and effectively update their skills and knowledge. Wiley supports students in this endeavor through the development and distribution of these courses as Microsoft's official academic publisher.

Today educational publishing requires attention to providing quality print and robust electronic content. By integrating Microsoft Official Academic Course products, *WileyPLUS*, and Microsoft certifications, we are better able to deliver efficient learning solutions for students and teachers alike.

Joseph Heider

General Manager and Senior Vice President

Preface

Welcome to the Microsoft Official Academic Course (MOAC) program for Microsoft .NET Fundamentals. MOAC represents the collaboration between Microsoft Learning and John Wiley & Sons, Inc. publishing company. Microsoft and Wiley teamed up to produce a series of textbooks that deliver compelling and innovative teaching solutions to instructors and superior learning experiences for students. Infused and informed by in-depth knowledge from the creators of Microsoft products, and crafted by a publisher known worldwide for the pedagogical quality of its products, these textbooks maximize skills transfer in minimum time. Students are challenged to reach their potential by using their new technical skills as highly productive members of the workforce.

Because this knowledge base comes directly from Microsoft, creator of the Microsoft Certified IT Professional (MCITP), Microsoft Certified Technology Specialist (MCTS), and Microsoft Technology Associate (MTA) exams (www.microsoft.com/learning/certification), you are sure to receive the topical coverage that is most relevant to students' personal and professional success. Microsoft's direct participation not only assures you that MOAC textbook content is accurate and current; it also means that students will receive the best instruction possible to enable their success on certification exams and in the workplace.

■ The Microsoft Official Academic Course Program

The *Microsoft Official Academic Course* series is a complete program for instructors and institutions to prepare and deliver great courses on Microsoft software technologies. With MOAC, we recognize that, because of the rapid pace of change in the technology and curriculum developed by Microsoft, there is an ongoing set of needs beyond classroom instruction tools for an instructor to be ready to teach the course. The MOAC program endeavors to provide solutions for all these needs in a systematic manner in order to ensure a successful and rewarding course experience for both instructor and student—technical and curriculum training for instructor readiness with new software releases; the software itself for student use at home for building hands-on skills, assessment, and validation of skill development; and a great set of tools for delivering instruction in the classroom and lab. All are important to the smooth delivery of an interesting course on Microsoft software, and all are provided with the MOAC program. We think about the model below as a gauge for ensuring that we completely support you in your goal of teaching a great course. As you evaluate your instructional materials options, you may wish to use the model for comparison purposes with available products.

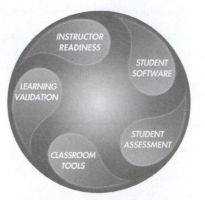

www.wiley.com/college/microsoft *or*
call the MOAC Toll-Free Number: 1+(888) 764-7001 (U.S. & Canada only)

▪ Pedagogical Features

The MOAC textbook for Microsoft .NET Fundamentals is designed to cover all the learning objectives for that MTA exam 98-372, which is referred to as its "objective domain." The Microsoft Technology Associate (MTA) exam objectives are highlighted throughout the textbook. Many pedagogical features have been developed specifically for *Microsoft Official Academic Course* programs.

Presenting the extensive procedural information and technical concepts woven throughout the textbook raises challenges for the student and instructor alike. The Illustrated Book Tour that follows provides a guide to the rich features contributing to *Microsoft Official Academic Course* program's pedagogical plan. Following is a list of key features in each lesson designed to prepare students for success as they continue in their IT education, on the certification exams, and in the workplace:

* Each lesson begins with an **Exam Objective Matrix**. More than a standard list of learning objectives, the Exam Objective Matrix correlates each software skill covered in the lesson to the specific exam objective domain.

* Concise and frequent **Step-by-Step** instructions teach students new features and provide an opportunity for hands-on practice. Numbered steps give detailed, step-by-step instructions to help students learn software skills.

* **Illustrations:** Screen images provide visual feedback as students work through the exercises. The images reinforce key concepts, provide visual clues about the steps, and allow students to check their progress.

* **Key Terms:** Important technical vocabulary is listed with definitions at the beginning of the lesson. When these terms are used later in the lesson, they appear in bold italic type and are defined. The Glossary contains all of the key terms and their definitions.

* Engaging point-of-use **Reader Aids**, located throughout the lessons, tell students why this topic is relevant (*The Bottom Line*), provide students with helpful hints (*Take Note*). Reader Aids also provide additional relevant or background information that adds value to the lesson.

* **Certification Ready** features throughout the text signal students where a specific certification objective is covered. They provide students with a chance to check their understanding of that particular MTA objective and, if necessary, review the section of the lesson where it is covered. MOAC offers complete preparation for MTA certification.

* **End-of-Lesson Questions:** The Knowledge Assessment section provides a variety of multiple-choice, true-false, matching, and fill-in-the-blank questions.

* **End-of-Lesson Exercises:** Competency Assessment case scenarios and Proficiency Assessment case scenarios are projects that test students' ability to apply what they've learned in the lesson.

■ Lesson Features

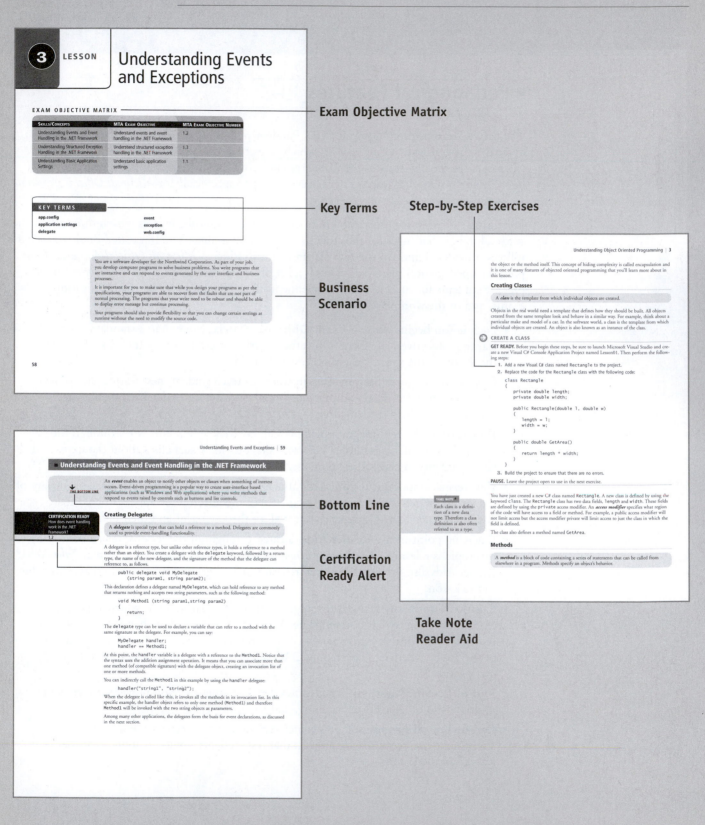

Exam Objective Matrix

Key Terms

Step-by-Step Exercises

Business Scenario

Bottom Line

Certification Ready Alert

Take Note Reader Aid

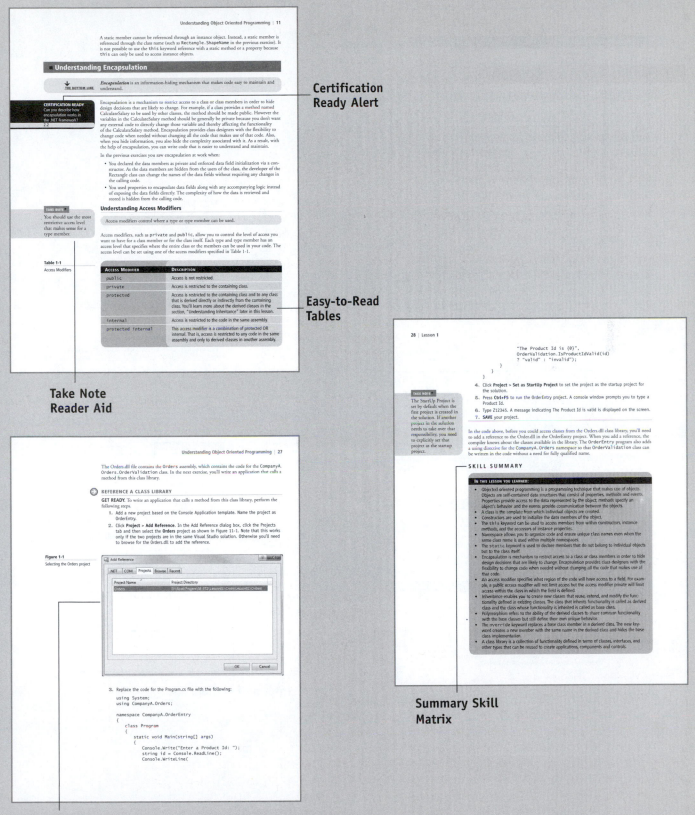

Certification
Ready Alert

Easy-to-Read
Tables

Take Note
Reader Aid

Screen Images

Summary Skill
Matrix

Knowledge Assessment Questions

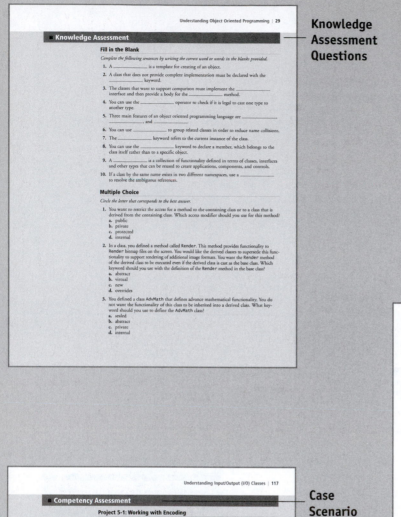

Case Scenario

Informative Diagrams

Conventions and Features Used in This Book

This book uses particular fonts, symbols, and heading conventions to highlight important information or to call your attention to special steps. For more information about the features in each lesson, refer to the Illustrated Book Tour section.

CONVENTION	MEANING
↓ THE BOTTOM LINE	This feature provides a brief summary of the material to be covered in the section that follows.
CLOSE	Words in all capital letters indicate instructions for opening, saving, or closing files or programs. They also point out items you should check or actions you should take.
CERTIFICATION READY	This feature signals the point in the text where a specific certification objective is covered. It provides you with a chance to check your understanding of that particular MTA objective and, if necessary, review the section of the lesson where it is covered.
TAKE NOTE*	Reader aids appear in shaded boxes found in your text. *Take Note* provides helpful hints related to particular tasks or topics.
X REF	These notes provide pointers to information discussed elsewhere in the textbook or describe interesting features of Microsoft .NET Framework that are not directly addressed in the current topic or exercise.
Alt + Tab	A plus sign (+) between two key names means that you must press both keys at the same time. Keys that you are instructed to press in an exercise will appear in the font shown here.
Example	Key terms appear in bold italic.

Instructor Support Program

The *Microsoft Official Academic Course* programs are accompanied by a rich array of resources that incorporate the extensive textbook visuals to form a pedagogically cohesive package. These resources provide all the materials instructors need to deploy and deliver their courses. Resources available online for download include:

- **DreamSpark Premium** is designed to provide the easiest and most inexpensive developer tools, products, and technologies available to faculty and students in labs, classrooms, and on student PCs. A free 3-year membership is available to qualified MOAC adopters.

  Note: Microsoft Visio, Microsoft Visual Studio, and Microsoft Expression can be downloaded from DreamSpark Premium for use by students in this course.

- The **Instructor Guides** contains Solutions to all the textbook exercises and Syllabi for various term lengths. The Instructor Guides also includes chapter summaries and lecture notes. The Instructor's Guide is available from the Book Companion site (http://www.wiley.com/college/microsoft).

- The **Test Bank** contains hundreds of questions in multiple-choice, true-false, short answer, and essay formats, and is available to download from the Instructor's Book Companion site (www.wiley.com/college/microsoft). A complete answer key is provided.

- A complete set of **PowerPoint presentations and images** are available on the Instructor's Book Companion site (http://www.wiley.com/college/microsoft) to enhance classroom presentations. Approximately 50 PowerPoint slides are provided for each lesson. Tailored to the text's topical coverage and Skills Matrix, these presentations are designed to convey key concepts addressed in the text. All images from the text are on the Instructor's Book Companion site (http://www.wiley.com/college/microsoft). You can incorporate them into your PowerPoint presentations, or create your own overhead transparencies and handouts. By using these visuals in class discussions, you can help focus students' attention on key elements of technologies covered and help them understand how to use it effectively in the workplace.

- When it comes to improving the classroom experience, there is no better source of ideas and inspiration than your fellow colleagues. The **Wiley Faculty Network** connects teachers with technology, facilitates the exchange of best practices, and helps to enhance instructional efficiency and effectiveness. Faculty Network activities include technology training and tutorials, virtual seminars, peer-to-peer exchanges of experiences and ideas, personal consulting, and sharing of resources. For details visit www.WhereFacultyConnect.com.

DREAMSPARK PREMIUM—FREE 3-YEAR MEMBERSHIP AVAILABLE TO QUALIFIED ADOPTERS!

DreamSpark Premium is designed to provide the easiest and most inexpensive way for universities to make the latest Microsoft developer tools, products, and technologies available in labs, classrooms, and on student PCs. DreamSpark Premium is an annual membership program for departments teaching Science, Technology, Engineering, and Mathematics (STEM) courses. The membership provides a complete solution to keep academic labs, faculty, and students on the leading edge of technology.

Software available in the DreamSpark Premium program is provided at no charge to adopting departments through the Wiley and Microsoft publishing partnership.

And tools that professors can use to engage and inspire today's technology students.

Contact your Wiley rep for details.

For more information about the DreamSpark Premium program, go to:

https://www.dreamspark.com/

Note: Microsoft Visio, Microsoft Visual Studio, and Microsoft Expression can be downloaded from DreamSpark Premium for use by students in this course.

■ Important Web Addresses and Phone Numbers

To locate the Wiley Higher Education Rep in your area, go to http://www.wiley.com/ college and click on the "*Who's My Rep?*" link at the top of the page, or call the MOAC Toll Free Number: 1 + (888) 764-7001 (U.S. & Canada only).

To learn more about becoming a Microsoft Certified Technology Specialist and exam availability, visit www.microsoft.com/learning/mcp/mcp.

Student Support Program

▪ Additional Resources

Book Companion Web Site (www.wiley.com/college/microsoft)

The students' book companion site for the MOAC series includes any resources, exercise files, and Web links that will be used in conjunction with this course.

Wiley Desktop Editions

Wiley MOAC Desktop Editions are innovative, electronic versions of printed textbooks. Students buy the desktop version for up to 40% off the U.S. price of the printed text, and get the added value of permanence and portability. Wiley Desktop Editions provide students with numerous additional benefits that are not available with other e-text solutions.

Wiley Desktop Editions are NOT subscriptions; students download the Wiley Desktop Edition to their computer desktops. Students own the content they buy to keep for as long as they want. Once a Wiley Desktop Edition is downloaded to the computer desktop, students have instant access to all of the content without being online. Students can also print out the sections they prefer to read in hard copy. Students also have access to fully integrated resources within their Wiley Desktop Edition. From highlighting their e-text to taking and sharing notes, students can easily personalize their Wiley Desktop Edition as they are reading or following along in class.

▪ About the Microsoft Technology Associate (MTA) Certification

Preparing Tomorrow's Technology Workforce

Technology plays a role in virtually every business around the world. Possessing the fundamental knowledge of how technology works and understanding its impact on today's academic and workplace environment is increasingly important—particularly for students interested in exploring professions involving technology. That's why Microsoft created the Microsoft Technology Associate (MTA) certification—a new entry-level credential that validates fundamental technology knowledge among students seeking to build a career in technology.

The Microsoft Technology Associate (MTA) certification is the ideal and preferred path to Microsoft's world-renowned technology certification programs, such as Microsoft Certified Technology Specialist (MCTS) and Microsoft Certified IT Professional (MCITP). MTA is positioned to become the premier credential for individuals seeking to explore and pursue a career in technology, or augment related pursuits such as business or any other field where technology is pervasive.

MTA Candidate Profile

The MTA certification program is designed specifically for secondary and post-secondary students interested in exploring academic and career options in a technology field. It offers students a certification in basic IT and development. As the new recommended entry point for Microsoft technology certifications, MTA is designed especially for students new to IT and software development. It is available exclusively in educational settings and easily integrates into the curricula of existing computer classes.

MTA Empowers Educators and Motivates Students

MTA provides a new standard for measuring and validating fundamental technology knowledge right in the classroom while keeping your budget and teaching resources intact. MTA helps institutions stand out as innovative providers of high-demand industry credentials and is easily deployed with a simple, convenient, and affordable suite of entry-level technology certification exams. MTA enables students to explore career paths in technology without requiring a big investment of time and resources, while providing a career foundation and the confidence to succeed in advanced studies and future vocational endeavors.

In addition to giving students an entry-level Microsoft certification, MTA is designed to be a stepping stone to other, more advanced Microsoft technology certifications, like the Microsoft Certified Technology Specialist (MCTS) certification.

Delivering MTA Exams: The MTA Campus License

Implementing a new certification program in your classroom has never been so easy with the MTA Campus License. Through the purchase of an annual MTA Campus License, there's no more need for ad hoc budget requests and recurrent purchases of exam vouchers. Now you can budget for one low cost for the entire year, and then administer MTA exams to your students and other faculty across your entire campus where and when you want.

The MTA Campus License provides a convenient and affordable suite of entry-level technology certifications designed to empower educators and motivate students as they build a foundation for their careers.

The MTA Campus License is administered by Certiport, Microsoft's exclusive MTA exam provider.

To learn more about becoming a Microsoft Technology Associate and exam availability, visit www.microsoft.com/learning/mta.

▪ Activate Your FREE MTA Practice Test!

Your purchase of this book entitles you to a free MTA practice test from GMetrix (a $30 value). Please go to www.gmetrix.com/mtatests and use the following validation code to redeem your free test: **MTA98-372-GFDXD3YR6ZY9.**

The **GMetrix Skills Management System** provides everything you need to practice for the Microsoft Technology Associate (MTA) Certification.

Overview of Test features:

- Practice tests map to the Microsoft Technology Associate (MTA) exam objectives
- GMetrix MTA practice tests simulate the actual MTA testing environment
- 50+ questions per test covering all objectives
- Progress at own pace, save test to resume later, return to skipped questions
- Detailed, printable score report highlighting areas requiring further review

To get the most from your MTA preparation, take advantage of your free GMetrix MTA Practice Test today!

For technical support issues on installation or code activation, please email support@gmetrix.com.

Acknowledgments

■ MOAC MTA Technology Fundamentals Reviewers

We'd like to thank the many reviewers who pored over the manuscript and provided invaluable feedback in the service of quality instructional materials:

Yuke Wang, University of Texas at Dallas

Palaniappan Vairavan, Bellevue College

Harold "Buz" Lamson, ITT Technical Institute

Colin Archibald, Valencia Community College

Catherine Bradfield, DeVry University Online

Robert Nelson, Blinn College

Kalpana Viswanathan, Bellevue College

Bob Becker, Vatterott College

Carol Torkko, Bellevue College

Bharat Kandel, Missouri Tech

Linda Cohen, Forsyth Technical Community College

Candice Lambert, Metro Technology Centers

Susan Mahon, Collin College

Mark Aruda, Hillsborough Community College

Claude Russo, Brevard Community College

Heith Hennel, Valencia College

Adrian Genesir, Western Governors University

Zeshan Sattar, Zenos

Douglas Tabbutt, Blackhawk Technical College

David Koppy, Baker College

Sharon Moran, Hillsborough Community College

Keith Hoell, Briarcliffe College and Queens College—CUNY

Mark Hufnagel, Lee County School District

Rachelle Hall, Glendale Community College

Scott Elliott, Christie Digital Systems, Inc.

Gralan Gilliam, Kaplan

Steve Strom, Butler Community College

John Crowley, Bucks County Community College

Margaret Leary, Northern Virginia Community College

Sue Miner, Lehigh Carbon Community College

Gary Rollinson, Cabrillo College

Al Kelly, University of Advancing Technology

Katherine James, Seneca College

Brief Contents

Contents

Understanding Object-Oriented Programming

EXAM OBJECTIVE MATRIX

SKILLS/CONCEPTS	MTA EXAM OBJECTIVE	MTA EXAM OBJECTIVE NUMBER
Understanding Object-Oriented Programming	Understand Object-Oriented Concepts in the .NET Framework.	2.2
Understanding Encapsulation	Understand Object-Oriented Concepts in the .NET Framework.	2.2
Understanding Inheritance	Understand Object-Oriented Concepts in the .NET Framework.	2.2
Understanding Polymorphism	Understand Object-Oriented Concepts in the .NET Framework.	2.2
Understanding Interfaces	Understand Object-Oriented Concepts in the .NET Framework.	2.2
Understanding Namespaces	Understand .NET class hierarchies.	2.1
	Understand .NET namespaces.	2.3
Understanding and Creating Class Libraries	Understand and create class libraries.	2.4

KEY TERMS

abstract class

access modifier

accessors

assembly

auto implemented properties

base class

class

class library

constructor

derived class

encapsulation

events

inheritance

interface

method

namespace

new	property
object-oriented programming	sealed class
objects	static members
override	this
polymorphism	

You are a software developer for the Northwind Corporation and you work as part of a team to develop computer programs that solve complex business problems. Any programs that you write must be easy to understand and maintain over a long period of time. You need to develop programs using techniques that encourage code reuse, extensibility, and collaboration.

Rather than thinking about a program as a list of methods, you model real-world business concepts such as customers, products, and suppliers and interactions between them in your programs.

▪ Understanding Object-Oriented Programming

THE BOTTOM LINE

Object-oriented programming is a programming technique that makes use of objects. *Objects* are self-contained data structures that consist of properties, methods, and events. Properties specify the data represented by the object. Methods specify an object's behavior. *Events* provide communication between the objects.

Almost all code that you write in C# is associated with objects. In this section, you learn about the basics of object-oriented programming. In the following sections, you will learn about object-oriented programming concepts such as encapsulation, inheritance and polymorphism.

Understanding Object-Oriented Thinking

A software object is conceptually similar to a real-world object.

A great way to start thinking in an object-oriented way is to look at real-world objects such as cars, phones, music players, and so on. You'll notice that they all have state and behavior. For example, cars have state (a model name, a color, a current speed, a fuel level, and so on) and behavior (they accelerate, they brake, they change gears, and so on).

Some objects are simple while other objects are complex. Most complex objects (such as a car) are made up of smaller objects that, in turn, have their own state and behavior. Although a car is a complex object, you need to know only a few things in order to interact with the car. As you drive the car, you simply invoke a behavior (such as accelerating or braking); you don't need to know the internal details of what is working or how it's working.

A software object is conceptually similar to the real-world objects. An object stores its state in fields and exposes its behavior through methods. When a method is invoked on the object, you get a well-defined functionality without the need to worry about the inner complexity of the object or the method itself. This concept of hiding complexity is called encapsulation, and it is one of many features of objected-oriented programming that you'll learn more about in this lesson.

Creating Classes

A *class* is the template from which individual objects are created.

Objects in the real world need a template that defines how they should be built. All objects created from the same template look and behave in a similar way. For example, think about a particular make and model of a car. In the software world, a class is the template from which individual objects are created. An object is also known as an instance of the class.

 CREATE A CLASS

GET READY. Before you begin these steps, be sure to launch Microsoft Visual Studio and create a new Visual C# Console Application Project named Lesson01. Then perform the following steps:

1. Add a new Visual C# class named Rectangle to the project.

2. Replace the code for the Rectangle class with the following code:

```csharp
class Rectangle
{
    private double length;
    private double width;

    public Rectangle(double l, double w)
    {
        length = l;
        width = w;
    }

    public double GetArea()
    {
        return length * width;
    }
}
```

3. Build the project to ensure that there are no errors.

PAUSE. Leave the project open to use in the next exercise.

TAKE NOTE*

Each class is a definition of a new data type. Therefore a class definition is also often referred to as a type.

You have just created a new C# class named Rectangle. A new class is defined by using the keyword class. The Rectangle class has two data fields, length and width. These fields are defined by using the private access modifier. An *access modifier* specifies what region of the code will have access to a field or method. For example, a public access modifier will not limit access but the access modifier private will limit access to just the class in which the field is defined.

The class also defines a method named GetArea.

Methods

A *method* is a block of code containing a series of statements that can be called from elsewhere in a program. Methods specify an object's behavior.

A method defines the actions or operations supported by the class. A method is declared by specifying the access level, the return type, the name of the method, parentheses which may contain an optional list of parameters followed by a block of code enclosed in braces. The Rectangle class defines a single method named GetArea. For GetArea, the access level is public, the return type is double, the method name is GetArea, the parameter list is empty, and the block of code consists of a single return statement.

A method can return a value to the calling code. If a method does not intend to return any value, its return type is specified by using the void keyword. If the return type is not void, the method must use a return statement to return a value. The return statement terminates the execution of the method and returns the specified value to the calling code. The data type of the value returned from a method must match with the return type specified on the method's declaration line.

The return type of the GetArea method is double, which means that the GetArea method must return a value of the type double. The GetArea method satisfies this requirement by returning the expression length * width, which is a double value.

The following code defines an InitFields method that takes two parameters of type double and returns void:

```
public void InitFields(double l, double w)
{
    length = l;
    width = w;
}
```

The InitFields method takes two parameters and uses the parameter values to respectively assign the data field length and width. When a method's return type is void, the return statement with no value can be used. If a return statement is not used, as in the case of InitFields method, the method will stop executing when it reaches the end of the code block. The InitField method can be used to properly initialize the value of the data fields, but as you'll learn in the following section, constructors already provide you with a way of initializing a class.

Constructors

A *constructor* is a block of code used to initialize the data members of the object.

Constructors are special class methods that are executed when a new instance of the class is created. Constructors are used to initialize the data members of the object. Constructors must have exactly the same name as the class and they do not have a return type. Multiple constructors, each with a unique signature, can be defined for a class.

A constructor that takes no arguments is called as the default constructor as shown in the following code:

```
public Rectangle()
{
    length = 10;
    width  = 10;
}
```

If a class is defined without any constructor, an invisible default constructor is automatically generated that does absolutely nothing.

It is often useful to provide additional constructors to provide additional ways in which an object is initialized. The Rectangle class, defined earlier, provides only one way to create and initialize its object: by calling the constructor that accepts two parameters, both of the double data type:

```
public Rectangle(double l, double w)
{
    length = l;
    width = w;
}
```

Creating Objects

An object is created from the templates defined by classes.

A class provides a template for the data type, but a class is not something concrete that exists in memory and can hold data. For that, you'll need to instantiate an object of the class by invoking a class constructor.

⊙ **CREATE AN OBJECT**

GET READY. Use the console application project, Lesson01, which you created in the previous exercise, and then perform the following steps:

1. Modify the code of the Program class to the following:

```
class Program
{
    static void Main(string[] args)
    {
        Rectangle rect = new Rectangle(10.0, 20.0);
        double area = rect.GetArea();
        Console.WriteLine("Area of Rectangle: {0}",
            area);
    }
}
```

2. Select **Debug > Start Without Debugging**. A console window displays the area of the rectangle. When you select **Debug > Start Debugging**, the console window will close as soon as the program ends and you might not get a chance to review the output.

3. **SAVE** your project.

PAUSE. Leave the project open to use in the next exercise.

The Rectangle class provides only one way to construct an instance of the class: by calling a constructor with two arguments of the double data type. You create an object by using the new keyword followed by the call to the appropriate class constructor.

When the code executes, an object of Rectangle type is created in the memory. A reference to this memory is stored inside the rect variable. Later in this block of code, you can use rect to refer to and manipulate the object that was just created.

Using the object's reference, you can access the class members. For example, the code calls the GetArea method on the object and the value returned by the method is stored in the variable area. The data fields, length and width, of the object rect are not accessible here because they are marked as private in the class definition.

Properties

A ***property*** is a block of code that allows you to access a class data field in a safe and flexible way.

Properties are class members that can be accessed like data fields but can contain code (like a method can contain code). Properties are often used to expose the data fields of a class in a more controlled manner. For example, a private field can be exposed by using a public property.

The ***accessors*** of a property contain the code associated with reading for writing the property value. A property can have two accessors:

- The `get` accessor is used to return the property value.
- The `set` accessor is used to assign a new value to the property.

A property is often defined as public and by convention (it always has a name that begins with a capital letter). In contrast, the convention to name private data fields is to begin each name with a lowercase letter.

TAKE NOTE*

Properties are often referred to as "smart" fields because they can include code for checking data consistency or validity.

➔ CREATE A PROPERTY

GET READY. Use the project you saved in the previous exercise and perform the following steps:

1. Replace the code of the Rectangle class as follows. In this code, the constructor is removed and two properties are inserted:

```
class Rectangle
{
    private double length;
    private double width;

    public double Length
    {
        get
        {
            return length;
        }
        set
        {
            if (value > 0.0)
                length = value;
        }
    }
    public double Width
    {
        get
        {
            return width;
        }
        set
        {
            if (value . 0.0)
                width = value;
        }
    }
}
```

```
        public double GetArea()
        {
            return length * width;
        }
    }
```

2. Modify the code of the `Program` class to the following code:

```
class Program
{
    static void Main(string[] args)
    {
        Rectangle rect = new Rectangle();
        rect.Length = 10.0;
        rect.Width = 20.0;
        double area = rect.GetArea();
        Console.WriteLine(
            "Area of Rectangle: {0}", area);
    }
}
```

3. Select **Debug > Start Without Debugging**. A console window displays the area of the rectangle.

4. **SAVE** your project.

PAUSE. Leave the project open to use in the next exercise.

In this exercise, you have modified the `Rectangle` class to introduce two properties, `Length` and `Width`. The properties are very often defined with a public access modifier. If you closely look at the code for `Length`, the get accessor simply returns the value of the data field length. However, the set accessor checks for the new value being assigned to the property (using the `value` keyword) and modifies the data field length only if the value is positive. The private fields `length` and `width` are also called backing fields for the properties that respectively expose them.

The `Rectangle` class also does not declare any explicit constructor. In this case, the users of the class (the `Main` method) must use the default constructor and rely on properties to initialize the class data.

The `Main` method uses the properties `Length` and `Width` to set the data for the `rect` object. If you try to set either `Length` or `Width` to a negative value, it will be ignored; in that case, the data fields will still have their original values of 0.

While defining properties, you can exclude either the `get` or `set` accessor. If you don't include a `set` accessor, you don't provide a way to set the value of the property; as a result, you have a read-only property. In contrast, if you don't include the `get` accessor, you don't provide a way to get the value of the property. As a result, you have a write-only property.

> **TAKE NOTE***
>
> The usual programming pattern is that all the data fields of a class should be declared private, and that the access to these private fields should be provided via public properties that check the data values for validity.

Auto Implemented Properties

> *Auto implemented properties* enable you to quickly specify a property of a class without having to write code to `Get` and `Set` the property.

C# introduced auto-implemented properties beginning with version 3 to simplify the property declaration when there is no additional logic specified in the `get` and the `set` accessors.

For example, without the validation checks, the `Length` and `Width` properties are defined as follows:

```
private double length;
private double width;

public double Length
{
    get
    {
        return length;
    }
    set
    {
        length = value;
    }
}
public double Width
{
    get
    {
        return width;
    }
    set
    {
        width = value;
    }
}
```

With C# auto implemented properties, the simplified syntax for property declaration becomes:

```
public double Length { get; set; }
public double Width { get; set; }
```

In this case, the backing fields for the properties are defined behind the scene and are not directly accessible by the code.

The properties used with default constructors also simplify the creation and initialization of objects. For example, now the object can be created and initialized like this:

```
static void Main(string[] args)
{
    Rectangle rect = new Rectangle
        { Length = 10.0, Width = 20.0 };
    Console.WriteLine(
        "Area of Rectangle: {0}", rect.GetArea());
}
```

The this keyword

The *this* keyword can be used to access members from within constructors, instance methods, and the accessors of instance properties.

The `this` keyword is a reference to the current instance of the class. You can use `this` to refer to any member of the current object. For example, earlier in this chapter, the `Rectangle` class was written as follows:

```
class Rectangle
{
    private double length;
    private double width;

    public Rectangle(double l, double w)
    {
        length = l;
        width = w;
    }
    public double GetArea()
    {
        return length * width;
    }
}
```

But it could have been written as follows:

```
class Rectangle
{
    private double length;
    private double width;

    public Rectangle(double l, double w)
    {
        this.length = l;
        this.width = w;
    }

    public double GetArea()
    {
        return this.length * this.width;
    }
}
```

As displayed here, this was used within the constructor and the `GetArea` method to refer to the data fields of the current object of the `Rectangle` class. Although it isn't necessary to use `this` in this case, using it provides more flexibility in naming the method parameters. For example, you could define the constructor as follows:

```
public Rectangle(double length, double width)
{
    // the parameter names length and width
    // hide the class members length and
    // width in this scope
    this.length = length;
    this.width = width;
}
```

TAKE NOTE ✱ In C#, the characters // are used to add single-line comments to the code. The text following the // characters is ignored by the compiler. Multi-line comments start with the characters /* and end with the characters */.

Within the scope of the definition of the `Rectangle` constructor, using the names `length` and `width` will now refer to the parameter being passed. The name of the data fields have been shadowed and can only be accessed by using the `this` keyword.

Static members

Static members belong to the class itself rather than individual objects.

The class members (such as data fields, methods, and properties) discussed so far in this section all operate on individual objects. Such members are referred to as instance members because they can be used only after an instance of the class is created. In contrast, the static keyword is used to declare members that do not belong to individual objects but to the class itself. Such class members are referred to as *static members*. One common example of a static member is the familiar Main method that serves as the entry point for your program.

➡ CREATE A STATIC MEMBER

GET READY. Use the project you saved in the previous exercise and then perform the following steps:

1. Modify the code of the Rectangle class, as follows:

```
class Rectangle
{
    public static string ShapeName
    {
        get { return "Rectangle"; }
    }
    public double Length { get; set; }
    public double Width { get; set; }

    public double GetArea()
    {
        return this.Length * this.Width;
    }
}
```

2. Modify the code of the Program class to the following code:

```
class Program
{
    static void Main(string[] args)
    {
        Rectangle rect = new Rectangle
            { Length = 10.0, Width = 20.0 };

        Console.WriteLine("Shape Name: {0}, Area: {1}",
            Rectangle.ShapeName,
            rect.GetArea());
    }
}
```

3. Select **Debug > Start Without Debugging**. A console window displays the name and area of the rectangle.
4. **SAVE** your project.

PAUSE. Leave the project open to use in the next exercise.

When multiple instances of a class are created, a separate copy is created of each instance field but only one copy of the static field is shared by all instances.

A static member cannot be referenced through an instance object. Instead, a static member is referenced through the class name (such as `Rectangle.ShapeName` in the previous exercise). It is not possible to use the `this` keyword reference with a static method or a property because `this` can only be used to access instance objects.

■ Understanding Encapsulation

↓
THE BOTTOM LINE
Encapsulation is an information-hiding mechanism that makes code easy to maintain and understand.

CERTIFICATION READY
Can you describe how encapsulation works in the .NET Framework?
2.2

Encapsulation is a mechanism to restrict access to a class or class members in order to hide design decisions that are likely to change. For example, if a class provides a method named `CalculateSalary` to be used by other classes, the method should be made public. However, the variables in the `CalculateSalary` method should generally be private because you don't want any external code to directly change those variables and thereby affect the functionality of the CalculateSalary method. Encapsulation provides class designers with the flexibility to change code when needed without changing all the code that makes use of that code. Also, when you hide information, you also hide the complexity associated with it. As a result, with the help of encapsulation, you can write code that is easier to understand and maintain.

In the previous exercises you saw encapsulation at work when:

- You declared the data members as private and enforced data field initialization via a constructor. As the data members are hidden from the users of the class, the developer of the `Rectangle` class can change the names of the data fields without requiring any changes in the calling code.
- You used properties to encapsulate data fields along with any accompanying logic instead of exposing the data fields directly. The complexity of how the data is retrieved and stored is hidden from the calling code.

Understanding Access Modifiers

TAKE NOTE *
You should use the most restrictive access level that makes sense for a type member.

Access modifiers control where a type or type member can be used.

Access modifiers, such as `private` and `public`, allow you to control the level of access you want to have for a class member or for the class itself. Each type and type member has an access level that specifies where the entire class or the members can be used in your code. The access level can be set using one of the access modifiers specified in Table 1-1.

Table 1-1

Access Modifiers

ACCESS MODIFIER	DESCRIPTION
`public`	Access is not restricted.
`private`	Access is restricted to the containing class.
`protected`	Access is restricted to the containing class and to any class that is derived directly or indirectly from the containing class. You'll learn more about the derived classes in the section, "Understanding Inheritance" later in this lesson.
`internal`	Access is restricted to the code in the same assembly.
`protected internal`	This access modifier is a combination of protected OR internal. That is, access is restricted to any code in the same assembly and only to derived classes in another assembly.

TAKE NOTE *

When the C# code is complied, the output executable code contained within a dll or an exe file is also called an assembly. An **assembly** is a unit of executable code that can be independently versioned and installed.

The `internal` access modifier is the default for a class if no access modifier is specified. The `Rectangle` class defined in previous exercise defaults to having an internal access. Accessibility of a nested class cannot be less restrictive than the accessibility of the containing class.

■ Understanding Inheritance

↓
THE BOTTOM LINE

Inheritance is an object-oriented programming technique that allows you to create new classes that reuse and extend functionality of existing classes.

CERTIFICATION READY
What does inheritance enable you to do?
2.2

Inheritance enables you to create new classes that reuse, extend, and modify the functionality defined in existing classes. The class that inherits functionality is a **derived class** and the class whose functionality is inherited is a **base class**.

TAKE NOTE *

Unlike classes, the `struct` does not support inheritance. For more information about `struct`, refer to Lesson 2.

Creating Derived Classes

The derived classes inherit all the functionality from the base class and can also define additional features that make them different from the base class.

Let's say that we want to create a set of classes that describes polygons (such as rectangles or triangles). These classes will have some common properties, such as `width` and `length`. For this case, you can create a base class `Polygon` with the `Width` and `Length` properties and the derived classes `Rectangle` and `Triangle` will inherit these properties while providing their own functionality. The following exercise explains this in more details.

➡ **CREATE A DERIVED CLASS**

GET READY. Use the project you saved in the previous exercise and perform the following steps:

1. Add a new `Polygon` class as follows:

```
class Polygon
{
    public double Length { get; protected set; }
    public double Width { get; protected set; }
}
```

2. Modify the `Rectangle` class as follows:

```
class Rectangle : Polygon
{
    public Rectangle(double length, double width)
    {
```

```
        Length = length;
        Width = width;
    }
    public double GetArea()
    {
        return Width * Length;
    }
}
```

3. Modify the code of the Main method as follows:

```
static void Main(string[] args)
{
    Rectangle rect = new Rectangle(10, 20);
    Console.WriteLine(
        "Width={0}, Length={1}, Area = {2}",
        rect.Width, rect.Length, rect.GetArea());
}
```

4. Select **Debug > Start Without Debugging**. A console window displays the area of the width, length, and area of the rectangle.

5. **SAVE** your project.

PAUSE. Leave the project open to use in the next exercise.

To define a derived class, put a colon after the derived class name followed by the name of the base class. Here the Polygon class is the base class for the Rectangle class.

The properties Length and Width in the Polygon class are declared with a protected access modifier for the set accessor. This means that access to the set accessor is available only inside the Polygon class and its derived classes. You can still get the value of the Length and Width properties in the Main method but you'll get an error if you attempt to assign a value to these properties.

The Rectangle class inherits all the non-private data and behavior from the Polygon class. In addition, the Rectangle class defines additional functionality (GetArea method) that is not available in the base class.

Creating Abstract Classes and Sealed Classes

An *abstract class* provides a common definition of the base class that can be shared by multiple derived classes. A *sealed class* provides complete definition for a class but cannot be used as a base class.

In the previous exercise, you defined a GetArea method on the Rectangle class. Suppose you want to create another class, Triangle, that is of the Polygon type. Now, you'll need a GetArea method in the Triangle class that will calculate a triangle's area.

Often, the base classes act as the repository of the common functionality. In the case of Polygon, the polygon itself won't know how to calculate the area without the knowledge of the shape type. But in general, we can expect all classes of Polygon type to have an ability to calculate their areas. Such expectations can be rolled over to the base class with the help of the abstract and override keywords.

→ **CREATE AN ABSTRACT CLASS**

GET READY. Use the project you saved in the previous exercise and then perform the following steps.

1. Modify the Polygon class as follows:

```
abstract class Polygon
{
    public double Length { get; protected set; }
    public double Width { get; protected set; }

    abstract public double GetArea();
}
```

2. Modify the Rectangle class as follows:

```
class Rectangle : Polygon
{
    public Rectangle(double length, double width)
    {
        Length = length;
        Width = width;
    }
    public override double GetArea()
    {
        return Width * Length;
    }
}
```

3. No modification to the Main method is needed. Select **Debug > Start Without Debugging**. A console window displays the width, length, and the area of the rectangle.

4. **SAVE** your project.

PAUSE. Leave the project open to use in the next exercise.

TAKE NOTE *

You cannot create instances of an abstract class.

This version of the Polygon class defines a method named GetArea. The main reason for including this method in the base class is that now the base class can provide a common template of functionality for the derived classes. But as we discussed, the Polygon base class doesn't know enough to calculate the area of the shape. This situation can be handled by marking the method as abstract. An abstract method just provides a definition but does not provide any implementation (the method body). If any of the members of the class are abstract, the class itself needs to be marked as abstract. An abstract class cannot be instantiated.

The derived classes can provide an implementation of the abstract class to create a concrete class (a non-abstract class). The derived classes provide an implementation of an abstract method by overriding it in a derived class. For example, in Step 2, the Rectangle class overrides the abstract GetArea method of the base class and provides full implementation. As a result, the Rectangle class is no longer an abstract class; it can be instantiated directly.

The sealed classes, in contrast, are defined when your implementation is complete and you do not want a class to be inherited. A sealed class can be created by using the sealed keyword:

```
sealed class Square : Rectangle
{
    // class members here
}
```

Because `Square` is a sealed class, it cannot be a used as a base class. It is also possible to mark selected class members as sealed to avoid them being overridden in a derived class. For example, you can say:

```
sealed public override double GetArea()
{
    return Width * Width;
}
```

This declaration ensures that the `GetArea` method cannot be overridden in a derived class.

Inheriting from the Object Class

The `Object` class is the ultimate base class of all the classes in the .NET Framework.

All classes in the .NET Framework directly or indirectly inherit from the `Object` class. For example, when you declared the following class earlier in this lesson:

```
class Polygon
{
    public double Length { get; protected set; }
    public double Width { get; protected set; }
}
```

It was functionally equivalent to the following declaration:

```
class Polygon : Object
{
    public double Length { get; protected set; }
    public double Width { get; protected set; }
}
```

But you are not required to declare the `Polygon` class in the latter way because inheritance from the `Object` class is implicitly assumed. As part of this inheritance, a derived class can override the methods of the `Object` class. Two of the most common methods to override are:

- `Equals`: Supports comparison between two objects. Returns `true` if the two objects have the same value.
- `ToString`: Returns a string representation of the class. By default, returns the full name of the class. It is often useful to override this method so that it returns a string representation of the current state of the object.

The following example shows how you can override the `ToString` method in the `Rectangle` class:

```
class Rectangle : Polygon
{
    public Rectangle(double length, double width)
    {
        Length = length;
        Width = width;
    }

    public override double GetArea()
    {
        return Width * Length;
    }
    public override string ToString()
```

```
        {
            return String.Format(
                "Width = {0}, Length = {1}",
                Width, Length);
        }
    }
```

Casting Between Types

> The runtime allows you to convert an object to any of its base types. This process is also called as casting.

The derived classes have an "is-a" relationship with the base class. For example, we can say that the Rectangle is a Polygon. An object of the Rectangle class has effectively three data types in this case; the object is a Rectangle, the object is also a Polygon, and the object is also of type Object. As the previous section pointed out, everything implicitly inherits from System.Object.

The runtime allows you to cast an object to its class or to any of its base classes. For example you can say:

```
        Polygon p = new Rectangle(10, 20);
```

Here a new Rectangle object is created and is cast to its base type Polygon. C# doesn't require any special syntax here because a cast to base type is considered safe conversion. This is also referred to as an implicit cast.

Cast is also possible the other way round. For example, you can say:

```
        Object o = new Rectangle(10, 20);
        …

        Rectangle r = (Rectangle) o;
```

Here a Rectangle object is first assigned to an Object (the ultimate base class) and the resultant object is then cast back as a Rectangle. When the latter assignment happens, an explicit cast is required because you are converting a more general object to a less general object. An explicit cast is performed by placing the class name in parenthesis in front of an expression. The runtime checks if the value of o is compatible with the Rectangle class. If at execution time the value of variable o is not compatible with the Rectangle class, the runtime throws a System.InvalidCastException.

The is Operator

> To avoid runtime errors, such as the InvalidCastException, the is operator can be used to check if the cast is allowed before actually performing the cast:

```
    if (o is Rectangle)
    {
        Rectangle r = (Rectangle) o;
    }
```

Here the runtime will check the value of the object o. The cast statement is executed only if o contains a Rectangle object or something that inherits from Rectangle.

The as Operator

Another useful cast operator is the as operator. The as operator is similar to the cast operation, but in the case of as, if the type conversion is not possible, null is returned instead of raising an exception. For example, consider this code:

```
Rectangle r = o as Rectangle;
if (r != null)
{
    // do something
}
```

If at runtime it is not possible to cast the value of variable o to a rectangle, a value of null is assigned to the variable r. No exceptions will be raised.

■ Understanding Polymorphism

THE BOTTOM LINE

Polymorphism refers to the ability of the derived classes to share common functionality with the base classes but still define their own unique behavior.

CERTIFICATION READY
How does polymorphism work?
2.2

Let's say that you are developing an application that allows users to work with different kinds of polygons. You have a collection that contains different kinds of polygons, such as rectangles, triangles, and squares. Each polygon provides you with its own implementation of the Draw method. When you work with this collection, you don't necessarily know which exact shape you are working with, but you would like the correct Draw method to be invoked each time. Polymorphism enables you to do exactly that.

Using Polymorphism

Polymorphism allows the objects of the derived class to be treated at runtime as the object of the base class.

When a method is invoked at runtime, its exact type is identified and the appropriate method is invoked from the derived class. In the following exercise, you will learn how to use polymorphism.

 USE POLYMORPHISM

GET READY. Use the project you saved in the previous exercise and then perform the following steps:

1. Modify the Polygon class as follows:

```
class Polygon
{
    public virtual void Draw()
    {
        Console.WriteLine("Drawing: Polygon");
    }
}
```

2. Modify the Rectangle class as follows:

```
class Rectangle : Polygon
{
    public override void Draw()
    {
        Console.WriteLine("Drawing: Rectangle");
    }
}
```

3. Add a new class, Triangle, as follows:

```
class Triangle : Polygon
{
    public override void Draw()
    {
        Console.WriteLine("Drawing: Triangle");
    }
}
```

4. Modify the Main method as follows:

```
static void Main(string[] args)
{
    List<Polygon> polygons = new List<Polygon> ();
    polygons.Add(new Polygon());
    polygons.Add(new Rectangle());
    polygons.Add(new Triangle());

    foreach (Polygon p in polygons)
    {
        p.Draw();
    }
}
```

5. Select **Debug > Start Without Debugging**. A console window displays the drawing message for each polygon.

6. **SAVE** your project.

PAUSE. Leave the project open to use in the next exercise.

In this exercise, the definitions of the Polygon and the Rectangle class are simplified to emphasize the concept of polymorphism. The base class provides a single Draw method. The important thing to note here is the virtual keyword, which allows the derived classes to override the method. This is in contrast to the abstract keyword from the earlier examples in which the base class is not providing a default definition of the method.

Both the Rectangle and Triangle classes override the base class Draw method with their own definition by using the override keyword. The Main method generates the following output:

```
Drawing: Polygon
Drawing: Rectangle
Drawing: Triangle
```

The List<Polygon> data type is capable of storing a collection of objects that are of the Polygon type or types that derive from Polygon. The foreach loop is iterating over a collection of Polygon objects. The underlying type of the first object is Polygon, but the second and third objects in the collection are actually Rectangle and Triangle objects that just happen to be cast as a Polygon. The runtime will look at the actual underlying type and invoke the overridden method from the derived class. That's the reason the derived class version of the Draw method is called for both rectangle and triangle objects.

Using the override and new Keywords

> The *override* keyword replaces a base class member in a derived class. The *new* keyword creates a new member with the same name in the derived class and hides the base class implementation.

When the base class defines a virtual member, the derived class has two options to handle it. The derived class can use either the override keyword or the new keyword. The override keyword takes priority over the base class definition of the member. The object of the derived class will call the overridden member instead of the base class member.

If the new keyword is used, a new definition of the member is created and the base class member is hidden. However, if the derived class is cast to an instance of the base class, the hidden members of the class can still be called.

 USE NEW OR OVERRIDE METHODS

GET READY. Perform the following steps to use the new and override methods from the base class.

1. Modify the Triangle method from the previous exercise to the following:

```
class Triangle : Polygon
{
    public new void Draw()
    {
        Console.WriteLine("Drawing: Triangle");
    }
}
```

2. Modify the code in the Main method from the previous exercise to the following:

```
Triangle t = new Triangle();
t.Draw();

Polygon p = t;
p.Draw();
```

3. Select **Debug > Start Without Debugging**. A console window displays the following output:

```
Drawing: Triangle
Drawing: Polygon
```

4. **SAVE** your project.

PAUSE. Leave the project open to use in the next exercise.

When Draw method is directly invoked on the object of the derived class, the new version of the method is used. However, if the method is executed when the derived class is cast as a base class, the hidden base class version of the Draw method is executed.

> The System.Object class provides a ToString method. By convention, you should use this method to return the human readable representation for a class. When you create your types, it is good practice to override this method to return readable information about the objects.

■ Understanding Interfaces

An *interface* is used to establish contracts through which the objects interact with each other without knowing the implementation details.

Interfaces are defined by using the `interface` keyword. An `interface` definition consists of a set of signatures for methods, properties, delegates, events, or indexers (delegates and events are discussed in Lesson 3). An interface definition cannot consist of any data fields or any implementation details such as method bodies.

A common interface already defined in the `System` namespace is the `IComparable` namespace. This is a simple interface defined as follows:

```
interface IComparable
{
    int CompareTo(object obj);
}
```

 TAKE NOTE*

By convention, all interfaces defined in the .NET Framework begin with a capital I. Although you are free to name your interfaces as you wish, it is best to follow with the framework convention.

Using the IComparable Interface

The `IComparable` interface has a single method (`CompareTo`) that accepts an object and returns an `int`. The return value of this method indicates the result of comparing the given parameter with the current object.

According to the documentation of the `CompareTo` method:

- If the instance is equal to the parameter, `CompareTo` returns `0`.
- A positive value is returned if the parameter value is less than the instance or if the parameter is null.
- If the parameter value is more than the instance, a negative value is returned.
- If the parameter is not of the compatible type, an `ArgumentException` is thrown.

How does `IComparable` decide how to compare two `Rectangle` objects or two `Employee` objects? It doesn't. The classes that are interested in such comparison must implement the `IComparable` interface by providing a method body for the `CompareTo` method. Each class that implements `IComparable` is free to provide its own custom comparison logic inside the `CompareTo` method. In fact, `IComparable` is commonly used by the .NET Framework class libraries for common tasks (such as sorting) in which a comparison operation is needed.

→ **USE THE ICOMPARABLE INTERFACE**

GET READY. Use the project you saved in the previous exercise and then perform the following steps.

1. Modify the Rectangle class as follows:

```
class Rectangle : Polygon, IComparable
{
    public double Length { get; set; }
    public double Width { get; set; }
```

```
        public override void Draw()
        {
            Console.WriteLine("Drawing: Rectangle");
        }
        public double GetArea()
        {
            return Length * Width;
        }
        public int CompareTo(object obj)
        {
            if (obj == null)
                return 1;
            if (!(obj is Rectangle))
                throw new ArgumentException();

            Rectangle target = (Rectangle)obj;
            double diff = this.GetArea() - target.GetArea();

            if (diff == 0)
                return 0;
            else if (diff > 0)
                return 1;
            else return -1;
        }
    }
```

2. Modify the Main method as follows:

```
static void Main(string[] args)
{
    Rectangle rect1 = new Rectangle
        { Length = 10, Width = 20 };
    Rectangle rect2 = new Rectangle
        { Length = 100, Width = 200 };

    Console.WriteLine(rect1.CompareTo(rect2));
}
```

3. Select **Debug > Start Without Debugging**. A console window displays the value (-1 as the area of rect1 is less than the area of rect2).

4. **SAVE** your project.

PAUSE. Leave the project open to use in the next exercise.

_____

The Rectangle class both derives from the Polygon class and implements the IComparable interface. A class that implements an interface must implement all the methods declared in the interface.

An interface is similar to an abstract class, but there are noticeable differences. An abstract class provides incomplete implementation while an interface provides no implementation at all.

A class can also implement multiple interfaces but is limited to inheriting from only a single base class. So, how do you decide whether to use an abstract class or an interface? One way you can decide is to check if an "is-a" relationship exists between the two concepts. For example, if an inheritance relationship exists between a SalariedEmployee and an Employee then you can use an abstract class to standardize common functionality among derived classes. In contrast, no "is-a" relation exists between an Employee and the IComparable. Therefore, the comparison functionality is best implemented as an interface.

■ Understanding Namespaces

THE BOTTOM LINE

As you write code in a business environment, you'll soon notice that you are dealing with a large number of classes. Some of these classes might be written by you, but many are written by others (such as developers working on other teams, vendors, and Microsoft includes many classes that are part of the .NET Framework itself). Namespaces provide a hierarchical way to organize code and create unique class name. In this section, you will learn how to create your own namespace hierarchy, and you will also learn how namespaces are used to organize the code in the .NET Framework class libraries.

CERTIFICATION READY
How does the .NET Framework logically organize classes?
2.1

CERTIFICATION READY
How are namespaces used in an application?
2.3

Namespace is a language element that allows you to organize code and create globally unique class names. Let's say that you create a class by the name `Widget`. Chances are that some other company can also ship code that contains a class by the name `Widget`. So how do you remove the ambiguity in the names? The solution is to organize the code within a namespace. A common convention is to use the company name in the namespace. For example, you can say:

```
namespace CompanyA
{
    public class Widget { … }
}
```

and

```
namespace CompanyB
{
    public class Widget { … }
}
```

The class from `namespace CompanyA` can be uniquely referred to by its fully qualified class name `CompanyA.Widget` while the other `Widget` can be uniquely identified as `CompanyB.Widget`.

It is possible to define a namespace in two or more declarations. In the following examples, the classes `WidgetA` and `WidgetB` are both part of the `CompanyA` namespace:

```
namespace CompanyA
{
    public class WidgetA { … }
}

namespace CompanyA
{
    public class WidgetB { … }
}
```

Additionally, the namespace declarations may be spread across multiple code files and projects. It doesn't matter if some of the classes of `CompanyA` namespace are compiled as part one project while the other classes of `CompanyA` namespace are compiled as part of another project. At compile time, the language compiler can look across multiple assemblies to create a unified view of a namespace hierarchy.

Access modifiers are not allowed on the namespace (namespace has not been explained yet) declarations, but a public access is implied for namespaces. The top-level classes (declared directly under a namespace) can be only `public` or `internal`.

Understanding Namespace Hierarchy

> Namespace hierarchies enable easy organization for a large number of classes.

Large software applications may have a lot of classes. For ease in understanding and reference, it is often helpful to organize classes in a hierarchical order of their functional areas. For example, CompanyA may organize the classes that deal with the accounts payable function as part of the CompanyA.Accounting.Payable namespace. This is a three-level hierarchy separated by dots. You can have classes at each of these levels: CompanyA, Accounting, and Payable. At the root level, you will often have more general classes and as you go deeper in the hierarchy, the classes get more specialized. You may have as many levels in the namespace hierarchy as you may need for organizing your classes.

The .NET Framework liberally uses namespaces to organize all of its classes. For example, the System namespace groups all the fundamental classes. The System.Data namespace organizes classes for data access. The System.Web namespace is used for Web-related classes, and so on.

With the use of namespaces, you might end up getting really long, fully qualified class names that may result in a very verbose program and a lot of typing. C# solves this inconvenience via the using directive. You can use the using directive at the top of the class file like this:

```
using System.Text;
```

Once you have included the using directive for a namespace, you don't need to fully qualify classes from that namespace in the code. For example, you can write something like this:

➔ USE NAMESPACES

GET READY. To make use of namespaces in your program, perform the following steps:

1. Add a new project based on the Visual C# Console Application template. Name the project as UsingNamespaces

2. Replace the code in the Program.cs file with the following code:

```csharp
using System;
using System.Text;
namespace CompanyA
{
    class Program
    {
        static void Main(string[] args)
        {
            StringBuilder sb =
                new StringBuilder("Sample");
            Console.WriteLine(sb.ToString());
        }
    }
}
```

3. Select **Debug > Start Without Debugging.** A console window displays the following output:

   Sample

4. **SAVE** your project.

PAUSE. Leave the project open to use in the next exercise.

In this code sample, the `Program` class itself is part of the `CompanyA` namespace. The fully qualified name of the Program class is `CompanyA.Program`. The `Program` class is using two classes, the `StringBuilder` class belongs to the `System.Text` namespace and the `Console` class belongs to the `System` namespace. If you don't write the `using` directives at the top of the code, you'll need to use fully qualified name of the class each time you use it, as in:

```
System.Text.StringBuilder sb =
    new System.Text.StringBuilder("Sample");
```

This might make your code very verbose. However, when you write using directives, you can write only the class name and the compiler will fully qualify the class names for you.

As previously discussed, in some situations, a class by the same name might exist in two different namespaces (say `CompanyA.Widget` and `CompanyB.Widget`). In such cases, there will be a conflict when you write code like this:

```
using CompanyA;
using CompanyB;
namespace CompanyA
{
    class Program
    {
        static void Main(string[] args)
        {
            Widget w = new Widget();
        }
    }
}
```

In this case, the compiler won't be able to automatically resolve the correct reference for `Widget` class (you will see a compilation error) because there is a `Widget` both in `CompanyA` and `CompanyB` namespace. You can resolve this ambiguity by changing the `using` directives to the following:

```
using CompanyA;
using CompanyBWidget = CompanyB.Widget;
```

Here the `using` directive defines a new non-ambiguous alias, `CompanyBWidget`, for the `CompanyB.Widget` class. Now, when you use just `Widget` in your code, the class will always get resolved to `CompanyA.Widget`. To refer to `CompanyB.Widget`, you will use the new alias `CompanyBWidget`.

TAKE NOTE*

To avoid possible ambiguity in references, do not use the same name for a namespace and a class within that namespace.

Using Common .NET Framework Namespaces

The .NET Framework uses namespaces to organize all of its classes and provides a large collection of classes that you can use in your code and benefit from the predefined functionality.

For ease in understanding and reference, these classes are organized into namespaces based on the function they provide. Table 1-2 lists some of the commonly used namespaces and the kind of functionality they provide.

Table 1-2

A sample of commonly used Namespaces in the .NET Framework

NAMESPACE	DESCRIPTION
System	Contains fundamental classes and base classes that define most common functionality
System.Data	Contains classes for accessing and managing data
System.IO	Contains classes that provide functionality for input and output
System.ServiceModel	Contains classes that help you build Windows Communication Foundation (WCF) applications
System.Web	Contains classes that help you build Web applications
System.Windows	Contains classes that help you build Windows applications
System.Xml	Contains classes for processing XML
System.Text	Contains classes for text encoding and string operations.
Microsoft.CSharp	Contains classes that support compilation and code generation for C# programming language

This is just a select list of namespaces to give you a basic idea. You can find a complete list of all namespaces and their classes on msdn.microsoft.com.

■ Understanding and Creating Class Libraries

↓
THE BOTTOM LINE

A *class library* is a collection of functionality defined in terms of classes, interfaces and other types that can be reused to create applications, components, and controls.

CERTIFICATION READY
How are class libraries created and what is the logic behind class libraries?

2.4

Let's say you are developing an order-entry application. This application consists of several forms where user has to enter data. Many of these forms require validation of the item number entered by the user. One way to program this is to write this validation functionality on every page. But this is not an ideal solution because this will require you to write same code over and over again. As discussed previously in this chapter, a much preferred solution is to write the functionality once in a class and then reuse that class on each page.

When you develop a complex business application, you will find several areas of functionality that you can package into reusable classes. A collection of these classes becomes a class library. However, when you use the word library it is implied that there is some organization that makes it easy for users to find and use exactly what they want. Just like a library won't keep its books in one giant pile, a software developer won't package a large collection of unrelated classes in a single file.

There are tools that you can use to create a good class library and two of the most important ones are:

- Namespaces
- Assemblies

You learned about namespaces in the previous section. When building an assembly, you can specify how code is packaged. For example, when you build a Visual Studio project, what you get in most cases is an assembly, which is usually in the form of a DLL or an EXE file.

Think of assemblies like this: if you package all the code in a single file, the users will not have flexibility to include the bits that they need; they are forced to take the whole thing or leave it altogether. So when you package your code, you should carefully plan to package related functionality together and unrelated functionality in separate assemblies. For example, if you are developing a Web application, in most cases, you don't need the functionality that comes as part of the System.Windows.dll assembly (which provides functionality for creating client application).

It is important to understand the distinction between namespace and assembly. Namespace enables you to organize classes into logical grouping. A namespace can span over one or more assemblies. An assembly, on the other hand, is more concrete; it specifies which code goes into which file on the disk. While it is common to put all the classes in a particular namespace as part of a single assembly, it is not necessary.

TAKE NOTE*

Assemblies are discussed in greater depth in Lesson 4, "Code Compilation and Deployment."

Creating a Class Library

Use the Class Library project template in Visual Studio to create a class library.

The following exercise shows you how to package classes into a class library. You'll create a class named OrderValidation, which is a part of the CompanyA.Orders namespace. The OrderValidation class provides a method called IsProductValid, which verifies if the given product id is valid or not.

Usually, a class library will have multiple classes and class members, but this simple exercise illustrates the process.

➔ CREATE A CLASS LIBRARY

GET READY. To package classes into a class library, perform the following steps.

1. Create a new project based on the Class Library template. Name the project as Orders.
2. Rename the file Class1.cs to OrderValidation.cs.
3. Replace the code in OrderValidation.cs (including the namespace definition) with the following:

```
namespace CompanyA.Orders
{
    public static class OrderValidation
    {
        public bool IsProductIdValid(string id)
        {
            if (id.Length == 6
                && id.StartsWith("Z"))
                return true;
            else
                return false;
        }
    }
}
```

4. Build the project. The Order.dll file is created in the project's output folder (usually bin/debug or bin/release).
5. **SAVE** your project.

Understanding Object-Oriented Programming | 27

The Orders.dll file contains the `Orders` assembly, which contains the code for the `CompanyA.Orders.OrderValidation` class. In the next exercise, you'll write an application that calls a method from this class library.

⊕ REFERENCE A CLASS LIBRARY

GET READY. To write an application that calls a method from this class library, perform the following steps.

1. Add a new project based on the Console Application template. Name the project as OrderEntry.

2. Click **Project > Add Reference**. In the Add Reference dialog box, click the Projects tab and then select the **Orders** project as shown in Figure 11-1. Note that this works only if the two projects are in the same Visual Studio solution. Otherwise, you'll need to browse for the Orders.dll to add the reference.

Figure 1-1

Selecting the Orders project

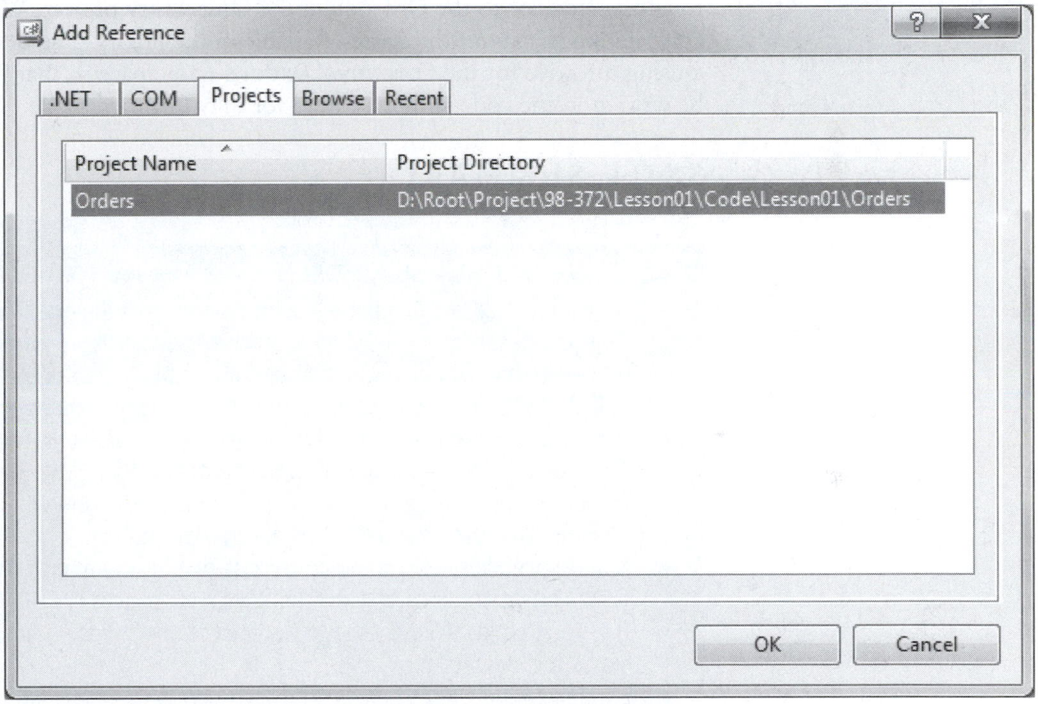

3. Replace the code for the Program.cs file with the following:

```
using System;
using CompanyA.Orders;

namespace CompanyA.OrderEntry
{
    class Program
    {
        static void Main(string[] args)
        {
            Console.Write("Enter a Product Id: ");
            string id = Console.ReadLine();
            Console.WriteLine(
```

```
            "The Product Id is {0}",
            OrderValidation.IsProductIdValid(id)
            ? "valid" : "invalid");
        }
    }
}
```

4. Click **Project > Set as StartUp Project** to set the project as the startup project for the solution.

5. Press **Ctrl+F5** to run the OrderEntry project. A console window prompts you to type a Product Id.

6. Type **Z12345**. A message indicating The Product Id is valid is displayed on the screen.

7. **SAVE** your project.

TAKE NOTE*

The StartUp Project is set by default when the first project is created in the solution. If another project in the solution needs to take over that responsibility, you need to explicitly set that project as the startup project.

In the code above, before you can access classes from the Orders.dll class library, you'll need to add a reference to the Order.dll in the OrderEntry project. When you add a reference, the compiler knows about the classes available in the library. The OrderEntry program also adds a using directive for the CompanyA.Orders namespace so that OrderValidation class can be written in the code without a need for fully qualified name.

SKILL SUMMARY

IN THIS LESSON YOU LEARNED:

- Object-oriented programming is a programming technique that makes use of objects. Objects are self-contained data structures that consist of properties, methods, and events. Properties provide access to the data represented by the object; methods specify an object's behavior and the events provide communication between the objects.
- A class is the template from which individual objects are created.
- Constructors are used to initialize the data members of the object.
- The this keyword can be used to access members from within constructors, instance methods, and the accessors of instance properties.
- Namespace allows you to organize code and ensure unique class names even when the same class name is used within multiple namespaces.
- The static keyword is used to declare members that do not belong to individual objects but to the class itself.
- Encapsulation is a mechanism to restrict access to a class or class members in order to hide design decisions that are likely to change. Encapsulation provides class designers with the flexibility to change code when needed without changing all the code that makes use of that code.
- An access modifier specifies what region of the code will have access to a field. For example, a public access modifier will not limit access, but the access modifier private will limit access within the class in which the field is defined.
- Inheritance enables you to create new classes that reuse, extend, and modify the functionality defined in existing classes. The class that inherits functionality is called a derived class, and the class whose functionality is inherited is called a base class.
- Polymorphism refers to the ability of the derived classes to share common functionality with the base classes but still define their own unique behavior.
- The override keyword replaces a base class member in a derived class. The new keyword creates a new member with the same name in the derived class and hides the base class implementation.
- A class library is a collection of functionality defined in terms of classes, interfaces, and other types that can be reused to create applications, components and controls.

Knowledge Assessment

Fill in the Blank

Complete the following sentences by writing the correct word or words in the blanks provided.

1. A _____ is a template for creating of an object.

2. A class that does not provide complete implementation must be declared with the _____ keyword.

3. The classes that want to support comparison must implement the _____ interface and then provide a body for the _____ method.

4. You can use the _____ operator to check if it is legal to cast one type to another type.

5. Three main features of an object-oriented programming language are _____, _____, and _____.

6. You can use _____ to group related classes in order to reduce name collisions.

7. The _____ keyword refers to the current instance of the class.

8. You can use the _____ keyword to declare a member, which belongs to the class itself rather than to a specific object.

9. A _____ is a collection of functionality defined in terms of classes, interfaces and other types that can be reused to create applications, components, and controls.

10. If a class by the same name exists in two different namespaces, use a _____ to resolve the ambiguous references.

Multiple Choice

Circle the letter that corresponds to the best answer.

1. You want to restrict the access for a method to the containing class or to a class that is derived from the containing class. Which access modifier should you use for this method?
   a. public
   b. private
   c. protected
   d. internal

2. In a class, you defined a method called `Render`. This method provides functionality to `Render` bitmap files on the screen. You would like the derived classes to supersede this functionality to support rendering of additional image formats. You want the `Render` method of the derived class to be executed even if the derived class is cast as the base class. Which keyword should you use with the definition of the `Render` method in the base class?
   a. abstract
   b. virtual
   c. new
   d. overrides

3. You defined a class `AdvMath` that defines advance mathematical functionality. You do not want the functionality of this class to be inherited into a derived class. What keyword should you use to define the `AdvMath` class?
   a. sealed
   b. abstract
   c. private
   d. internal

4. You need to provide query functionality to several of your classes. Each class's algorithm for query will likely be different. Not all the classes have an "is-a" relationship with each other. How should you support this functionality?
   a. Add to the query functionality to a base class with a public access modifier.
   b. Have all the classes inherit from an abstract base class and override base class method to provide their own query functionality.
   c. Have all the classes inherit from a base class that provides the query functionality.
   d. Create a common interface that is implemented by all the classes.

5. Which of the following class elements should be used to define the behavior of a class?
   a. Method
   b. Property
   c. Event
   d. Delegate

6. You are writing code for a class named Product. You need to make sure that the data members of the class are initialized to their correct values as soon as you create an object of the **Product** class. The initialization code should be always executed. What should you do?
   a. Create a static method in the **Product** class to initialize data members.
   b. Create a constructor in the **Product** class to initialize data members.
   c. Create a static property in the **Product** class to initialize data members.
   d. Create an event in the **Product** class to initialize data members.

7. You are creating a new class named **Square** that derived from the **Polygon** class. The **Polygon** class has the following code:

```
class Polygon
{
    public virtual void Draw()
    {
        // additional code...
    }
}
```

The Draw method in the Square class should provide new functionality but also hide the Polygon class implementation of the Draw method. Which code segment should you chose?
   a.

```
class Square : Polygon
{
    public override void Draw()
    {
        // additional code ...
    }
}
```

   b.

```
class Square : Polygon
{
    public new void Draw()
    {
        // additional code ...
    }
}
```

c.

```
class Square : Polygon
{
    public virtual void Draw()
    {
        // additional code ...
    }
}
```

d.

```
class Square : Polygon
{
    public static void Draw()
    {
        // additional code ...
    }
}
```

8. You are creating a new class named Rectangle. You write the following code:

```
class Rectangle : IComparable
{
    public double Length { get; set; }
    public double Width { get; set; }

    public double GetArea()
    {
        return Length * Width;
    }

    public int CompareTo(object obj)
    {
        // to be completed
    }
}
```

You need to complete the definition of the CompareTo method to enable comparison of the Rectangle objects. Which of the following code should you write?

a.

```
public int CompareTo(object obj)
{
    Rectangle target = (Rectangle)obj;
    double diff = this.GetArea() - target.GetArea();

    if (diff == 0)
        return 0;
    else if (diff > 0)
        return 1;
    else return -1;
}
```

b.

```
public int CompareTo(object obj)
{
    Rectangle target = (Rectangle)obj;
    double diff = this.GetArea() - target.GetArea();

    if (diff == 0)
        return 1;
    else if (diff > 0)
        return -1;
    else return 0;
}
```

c.

```
public int CompareTo(object obj)
{
    Rectangle target = (Rectangle)obj;

    if (this == target)
        return 0;
    else if (this > target)
        return 1;
    else return -1;
}
```

d.

```
public int CompareTo(object obj)
{
    Rectangle target = (Rectangle)obj;

    if (this == target)
        return 1;
    else if (this > target)
        return -1;
    else return 0;
}
```

9. You are writing code for a new method named `Process`:

```
void Process(object o)
{

}
```

The code receives a parameter of type `object`. You need to cast this object into the type `Rectangle`. At times, the value of `o` passed to the method might not be a valid `Rectangle` value. You need to make sure that the code does not generate any `System.InvalidCastException` errors while doing the conversions. Which of the following line of code should you use inside the `Process` method?

a. `Rectangle r = (Rectangle) o;`
b. `Rectangle r = o as Rectangle;`
c. `Rectangle r = o is Rectangle;`
d. `Rectangle r = (o != null) ? o as rectangle : (Rectangle) o;`

10. Which of the following C# features organizes code and creates globally unique types?
   a. assembly
   b. namespace
   c. class
   d. data type

Competency Assessment

Project 1-1: Creating Properties

You need to create a class named Product that represents a product. The class has a single property named Name. The users of the Product class should be able to get as well as set the value of the Name property. The user of the Product class should not be able to access any other data members of the Product class. How should you achieve this?

Project 1-2: Creating a Class Library

You are developing components of a complex accounting system. You need to develop two classes: Payable and Receivable. Both classes are part of the CompanyA.Accounting namespace. However, it should be possible to deploy each class separately. In other words, if you need only the code for the Payable class, you should not be required to package the code for the Receivable class as well. How should you achieve this?

Proficiency Assessment

Project 1-3: Overriding the ToString method

You are writing code for a ProductEx class. The ProductEx class contains the name and price of a product. You need to override the base class (System.Object) method ToString to provide information about the objects of the ProductEx class to the calling code. What code do you need to write in order to meet this requirement?

Project 1-4: Working with Virtual Methods

You are writing code for an Order class. The Order class contains a method named CalculateDiscount that returns a decimal type. The users of the Order class should be able to extend the behavior of the Order class and when they do so, the users should be able to override the behavior of the CalculateDiscount to change how the discount is calculated. What code should you write for the Order class in order to meet this requirement?

Understanding Data Types and Collections

EXAM OBJECTIVE MATRIX

SKILLS/CONCEPTS	MTA EXAM OBJECTIVE	MTA EXAM OBJECTIVE NUMBER
Understanding and Using Different Data Types in the .NET Environment	Understand and use different data types in the .NET Framework.	2.5
Understanding Arrays and Collections	Understand and use different data types in the .NET Framework.	2.5
Understanding Generics	Understand generics.	2.6

KEY TERMS

array

boxing

collection classes

constraints

contravariance

covariance

data type

generics

generic collection

intrinsic data types

memory safety

reference types

strongly typed language

struct

two-dimensional array

value types

verifiability

unboxing

You are a software developer for the Northwind Corporation. You work as part of a team to develop computer programs that solve complex business problems. Almost all programs that you write process data. To be effective at your work, you need to know the various data types that you can use in your programs. You need to understand how the data is stored in memory and the difference between the value types and reference types. You often need to work with a collection of data such as orders, items, and customers. You need to know how to use the collection classes to work with such data.

■ Understanding and Using Different Data Types in the .NET Environment

↓ THE BOTTOM LINE

Data types specify the kind of data that you work with in a program. The data type defines the size of memory needed to store the data and the kind of operation that can be performed on the data.

Each value in a C# program has a data type. The ***data type*** not only specifies the kind of data that a value represents but also specifies the kind of operations that are permitted on the value and how the value is stored in the computer memory.

C# provides a set of built-in data types, which are also called as intrinsic data types. In addition, you can also create your own custom types by using keywords such as `struct`, `class`, `interface` or `enum`. The .NET Framework also provides a large collection of complex pre-defined data types as part of its class libraries. In your C# program, depending on your specific requirements, you can use any of these available data types or define your own new custom data types.

C# is a ***strongly typed language***. That means the data types for variables, constants, literal values, method return values, and parameters must be known at the compile time. The compiler uses the data types to make sure that all operations performed in the code are type-safe. Type safety ensures that a program reads or writes the correct number of bytes from or to a memory location. Missing type safety, a program can potentially read a floating point number from a memory location assigned to an integer and thereby cause unpredictable results. For example, if you declare two variables of type `int`, the compiler will allow you to perform a subtraction operation with the variables. However, if the variables are of type `string` and if you try to perform subtraction, the compiler will generate an error because the subtraction operation is not defined between two strings.

Understanding Intrinsic Data Types

Intrinsic data types are the primitive data types for which the support is directly built into the programming language.

C# provides several built-in data types that you can use in your programs. Table 2-1 lists the intrinsic data type available in C# along with their equivalent .NET Framework type and the range of values represented by the type.

Also, as shown in Table 2-1, the C# intrinsic data type directly corresponds to a particular data type in the .NET Framework. As you will learn in more detail in Lesson 4, the .NET Framework language compilers (such as the C# compiler) compiles programs to a Common Intermediate Language (CIL) code that supports a Common Type System (CTS). This means that every data type that C# provides is just a wrapper around the basic data types defined by the .NET Framework. When a program is compiled, the type information is stored into the executable file as metadata. When the program executes, the runtime uses the type information stored in the metadata to provide type checks when allocating and reclaiming memory for variables and other data items.

You specify the data type for variables and constants that you declare in your program, as in the following examples:

```
// variables
int number = 12;
string name = "Anders";
// constants
const int radius = 10;
const double pi = 3.141;
// as return values and parameters.
long AddNumbers(int first, int second)
{
    long result = first + second;
    return result;
}
```

Table 2-1

The C# intrinsic data types

DATA TYPE	.NET FRAMEWORK TYPE	RANGE
bool	System.Boolean	true or false
byte	System.Byte	0 to 255
sbyte	System.SByte	–128 to 127
char	System.Char	A Unicode character
decimal	System.Decimal	–79228162514264337593543950335 to 79228162514264337593543950335
double	System.Double	–1.79769313486232e308 to 1.79769313486232e308
float	System.Single	–3.402823e38 to 3.402823e38
Int	System.Int32	–2,147,483,648 to 2,147,483,647
uint	System.UInt32	0 to 4,294,967,295
long	System.Int64	–9,223,372,036,854,775,808 to 9,223,372,036,854,775,807
ulong	System.UInt64	0 to 18,446,744,073,709,551,615
object	System.Object	An object
short	System.Int16	–32,768 to 32,767
ushort	System.UInt16	0 to 65,535
string	System.String	zero or more Unicode characters

Alternatively, you can use the var keyword to let the compiler infer the data type from the declaration, as shown in the following examples:

```
var number = 12;
var otherNumber = 12.0;
var name = "Anders";
```

In the preceding code, the compiler infers from the assignments that the type of the variable number is int, the variable otherNumber is double, and the type of the variable name is string. This also illustrates the danger of var if otherNumber was not supposed to be double. After a variable is declared, you can't change its type later in the program.

The C# types are interchangeable with their equivalent .NET Framework types. For example, you can declare an integer variable by using either of the following declarations and it will generate the same CIL code when the program is compiled:

```
int number = 12;
System.Int32 number = 12;
```

The GetType method, which is available on all types, can be used to find the runtime data type (as demonstrated in the following exercise).

FIND RUNTIME DATA TYPES

GET READY. To find the runtime data types for variables, perform the following steps.

1. Create a new C# Console Application project named RuntimeTypes. Save the project in a solution named Lesson02.

2. Modify the code of the Main method in the Program class as follows:

```
static void Main(string[] args)
{
    int number = 12;
    string name = "Anders";

    bool IsValid = true;
    double pi = 3.141;

    Console.WriteLine(
        "Runtime type for int: {0}",
        number.GetType());

    Console.WriteLine(
        "Runtime type for string: {0}",
        name.GetType());

    Console.WriteLine(
        "Runtime type for bool: {0}",
        IsValid.GetType());

    Console.WriteLine(
        "Runtime type for double: {0}",
        pi.GetType());
}
```

3. Run the project. The program output is displayed in a console window (see Figure 2-1).

Figure 2-1

Displaying the runtime type for variables

If you are running the project by clicking **Debug > Start Debugging**, the console window will close as soon as the program ends and you might not have chance to review the output. You can work around this issue by adding the following lines of code at the end of the Main method:

```
Console.WriteLine("Press any key to continue...");
Console.ReadKey();
```

Alternatively, you can run the program from the Windows command window or from within Visual Studio by clicking **Debug > Start Without Debugging**. In the latter case, you will have an opportunity to press a key before the output window closes.

Understanding Value Types and Reference Types

Value types directly store the value whereas *reference types* store only a reference to the actual value.

Every type in the .NET Framework is defined either as a value type or a reference type. The value types are called so because they directly store the data value within its memory location. The reference types, on the other hand, store only a reference to a memory location that contains the actual data.

A good way to understand how value types are different from reference types is to visualize how each is represented in the memory. Figure 2-2 shows how the value types are created in memory. When you create a variable of type `int`, a named memory location is created that you can use to store a value of type `int`. Initially when you don't explicitly assign a value, the default value of the data type (for `int` the default value is 0) is stored in the memory location. When an assignment is made, the memory address identified by the variable name is updated with the new value (which, in Figure 2-2, is 10).

Figure 2-2

Visualizing a value type in memory

Figure 2-3 shows the case of a reference type, the `string` data type. When you create a variable of type `string`, a memory location is created that will be identified by this name. However, this memory location is not going to contain the content of the string. This variable will store the memory address (a reference) of the location where the string is actually stored.

Figure 2-3

Visualizing a reference type in memory

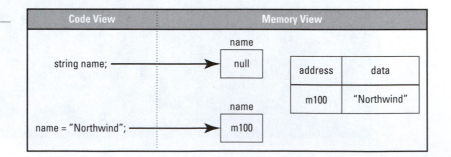

Initially, when no value is assigned, the variable will have the value of `null` (a null reference, or, in other words, this variable does not refer to a valid memory address). In the next statement when you say:

```
name = "Northwind";
```

The string "Northwind" is created at a particular memory location (to keep things simple, let's say the memory address is m100) and that memory address is stored in the variable. When it is time to retrieve the value of the variable `name`, the runtime will know that its contents are not stored in the variable itself but at the memory location pointed to by the variable.

Most intrinsic data types are value types. All the data types listed in Table 2-1 are value types except for **string** and **object**, which are reference types. In addition to the intrinsic types, the C# programming language provides one more way to create a value type and that is by using the **struct** keyword. The **struct** keyword is used to create user-defined types that consist of a group of related fields as follows:

```
public struct Point
{
    public double X, Y;
}
```

The **struct** can contain most of the elements that a class can contain, such as constructors, methods, properties, and so on. Unlike a class, a **struct** cannot inherit from another class or struct. Variables based on structs are value types as opposed to variables based on classes, which are reference types. Whenever you have a need for simple structured data that will be used often, structs might be a good option. But if you need to define behavior for the type by adding events and method, you should create a class.

TAKE NOTE✱

Structs are mostly used to create simple types. If you find yourself creating a very complex struct, you should consider using a class instead.

Reference types and value types behave differently when allocating and accessing memory.

COPY VALUE AND REFERENCE TYPES

GET READY. To understand how the copying of a variable works for a value type and a reference type, perform the following steps:

1. Add a new C# Console Application project to the Lesson02 solution. Name the project as ValueReference.

2. Replace the code in the Program file with the following code:

```
using System;
namespace ValueReference
{
    class Rectangle
    {
        public double Length { get; set; }
        public double Width { get; set; }
    }

    struct Point
    {
        public double X, Y;
    }

    class Program
    {
        static void Main(string[] args)
        {
            // Copying value type
            Point p1 = new Point();
            p1.X = 10.0;
            p1.Y = 20.0;
            Point p2 = p1;
            p2.X = 100.0;
            Console.WriteLine("p1.X = {0}", p1.X);
```

```
                // Copying reference type
                Rectangle rect1 = new Rectangle
                    { Length = 10.0, Width = 20.0 };

                Rectangle rect2 = rect1;
                rect2.Length = 100.0;

                Console.WriteLine("rect1.Length = {0}",
                    rect1.Length);
            }
        }
    }
```

TAKE NOTE*   You can create a struct without using the new operator. You can simply type `Point p1;` to create a variable of the **struct** type.

---

3. Run the project. A console window displays the values for `p1.X` and `rect1.Length`.

TAKE NOTE*   When you copy a reference type variable to another variable of the same type, only references are copied. As a result, both variables end up pointing to the same object.

The first part of this program creates a copy of the value type `Point` and the second half of the program creates a copy of the reference type `Rectangle`.

Let's first analyze how the copy of a value type is made. When the following statement is executed, a new variable `p2` is created in memory and its contents are copied from the variable `p1`:

```
    Point p2 = p1;
```

Both `p1` and `p2` have their own set of values available in their respective memory locations. So when the following statement is executed:

```
    p2.X = 100;
```

It only affects the value of `X` corresponding to the memory location of variable `p2`. The value of `X` for the variable `p1` remains unaffected.

Now let's analyze how the copy works between reference types. When the following statement is executed, a new variable `rect2` is created and, just like before, the contents of `rect1` are copied into the memory location of `rect2`.

```
    Rectangle rect2 = rect1;
```

But as the class `Rectangle` is a reference type, the content of variable `rect1` is actually a reference to a memory location that holds a `Rectangle` object. So after the above initialization, both `rect1` and `rect2` are now pointing to the same memory location and, in turn, the same `Rectangle` object. There is only one rectangle object in memory and both `rect1` and `rect2` are referring to it. The next statement modifies the `Length` of the `Rectangle` object:

```
    rect2.Length = 100.0;
```

This statement references the memory location pointed to by `rect2` (which happens to be the same memory location pointed to by `rect1`) and modifies the `Length` of the `Rectangle` object. Now, if you attempt to reference the same memory location via the `rect1` object, you get the modified object and the following code displays the value "rect1.Length = 100":

```
    Console.WriteLine("rect1.Length = {0}",
        rect1.Length);
```

TAKE NOTE *

The reference type variables are always allocated memory on the heap. The heap refers to the memory available to the program at runtime for dynamic memory allocation. In contrast, some data items can be created on the execution stack or the call stack. These items created on the stack are the method parameters and the local variable declared within a method. The stack memory is reclaimed when the stack unwinds (when a method returns for example). The memory allocated in the heap is automatically reclaimed by the garbage collector when the objects are not in use anymore (no other objects are holding a reference to them). The class objects are reference types and are allocated on heap. These objects have extra memory management overhead associated with them. When the objects are created, the memory must be allocated and then the garbage collector has to keep track of unused objects so that the allocated memory can be reclaimed. However, object references can be passed around between methods and classes without need for reallocation.

The value types such as struct are created on the stack. These values are discarded at the end of the code block in which the variable was defined. As there is no need to keep track of memory allocation for a long term, creating value types on stack is very efficient. However, each time you pass a value type to a method or another object, a copy of that value must be created.

Understanding Type Conversion and Casting

The data types specify rules for converting values in one type to another type. The conversion can be performed implicitly by the compiler or explicitly by using the `cast` operator. Not all data type conversions are permissible; when a conversion is not permitted, an `InvalidCastException` is thrown by the runtime.

A type conversion that does not cause data loss is performed automatically by the compiler. For example:

```
int number1 = 0;
double number2 = 0;
number1 = 12;
number2 = number1; // implicit conversion
```

A conversion that might cause data loss requires that the programmer explicitly use a `cast` operator is as follows:

```
number2 = 3.141;
number1 = (int) number2; // explicit cast
```

Here, conversion is possible but you'll lose information such as the value after the decimal point. Because of this possible risk of data loss, the compiler will generate an error unless the programmer uses the casting operation as shown above.

In many other cases, the data type conversion is not permissible whether the cast is used or not. For example, you can't assign a double value to a `bool` data type variable; not even if you use an explicit cast.

Understanding Boxing and Unboxing

Boxing is the process of converting a value type to the reference type. ***Unboxing*** is the process of converting a reference type to the value type.

The C# programming language has a unified type system. This means that a value of any type can be treated as an object. As mentioned previously, an object is a reference type. However, to enable this, some additional memory manipulation is involved at the runtime. For example, consider the following code:

```
int i = 10;
object o = i; //boxing
```

Because it is a value type, the value for the variable i is stored on the call stack. Because it is a reference type, the value for the variable o is stored on the heap memory. To store the integer value as an object, memory must be allocated in the heap and then the actual value will be copied from the stack to the heap memory and the location stored in the reference variable o. This process is called boxing.

The process of unboxing is the opposite of boxing. The value is copied from a heap memory location to the memory location in the call stack as follows:

```
object o = 10;
int i = (int) o; //unboxing
```

Notice that boxing is implicit; you need to explicitly cast for an unboxing operation, however. For unboxing to succeed, you must cast using the same type that was used for boxing. If you use a different data type, you might get InvalidCastException at runtime, as shown in the following code:

```
double p = 3.141;
object o = p; // boxing
int i = (int) o; //InvalidCastException
```

An exception is raised because the object o was allocated for storing a double value. So the unboxing operation must cast the value explicitly as a double. Once you have a double value, it can be further cast to an integer as follows:

```
int i = (int) (double) o; // valid cast
```

The way boxing and unboxing works, you need to be careful about certain operations. For example, consider the following code:

```
double p = 3.141;
object o1 = p;
object o2 = p;
Console.WriteLine(o1 == o2); // prints false
```

Here, o1 and o2 are two references pointing to separate memory locations. To compare the value pointed to by these references, use the following code:

```
Console.WriteLine(o1.Equals(o2)); // prints true
```

Also, be careful about the fact that boxing creates a copy of the value. Any change that you make to that copy doesn't affect the original value and vice-versa. This scenario is illustrated by the following code:

```
double p = 3.141;
object o1 = p;
p = 1.2;
Console.WriteLine(o1); // prints 3.141
```

■ Understanding Arrays and Collections

THE BOTTOM LINE

The .NET Framework *collection classes* provide data structures to store and manipulate a collection of items. An item in the collection can be anything such as a number, a string, a Customer object, and so on. These collection classes are defined as part of the System.Collections or System.Collections.Generic namespace.

CERTIFICATION READY
How are arrays and
collection classes used in
the .NET Framework?
2.5

The arrays are special type of collections declared by using a programming language construct. All arrays are internally derived from the `System.Array` class. In addition to storing items, all the collections provide methods and properties to help in manipulating the collection.

Using Arrays

An *array* is a collection of items stored in a contiguous memory location. Each item of an array can be accessed by using the array's index, which is unique for each item.

An array in C# is commonly used to represent a collection of items of the similar type. A sample array declaration is shown in the following code:

```
int[] numbers = { 11, 12, 13, 14, 15 };
```

This declaration creates an array identified by the name `numbers`. This array is capable of storing a collection of five integers. This declaration also initializes each of the array items respectively to the numbers 11 through 15. The `Length` property of an array returns the total number of items in the array. The expression `numbers.Length` will return a value of 4 as shown in the following code:

```
Console.WriteLine(numbers.Length);   //writes 4
```

Any array item can be directly accessed by using its index. In .NET Framework, array indexes are zero-based. This means that when you access the first element of an array, you use the index value of 0 and you use the index value of 1 to access the second element and so on.

To access an individual array item, use the name of the array followed by the index value enclosed in square brackets. For example, `numbers[0]` returns the value 11 from the above declared array and `numbers[4]` returns the value 15. It is illegal to access an array outside its defined boundaries. For example, you'll get an error if you try to access the array element `numbers[5]`.

In the following code, the first statement creates an array variable and the second statement initializes the variable with an array of 4 integers:

```
int[] numbers;
numbers = new int[4];
```

TAKE NOTE *

Arrays work best when the number of items in the collection is pre-determined and fast direct access to each item is required.

Initially, the variable numbers will be set to `null` because the array is not yet initialized. The second statement initializes the array by allocating a contiguous memory space big enough for storing 4 integers in the memory heap. The starting address in the memory allocation is stored in the array variable numbers, as shown in Figure 2-4. All the array elements are initialized in this case with the value `0` as that's the default value for an integer.

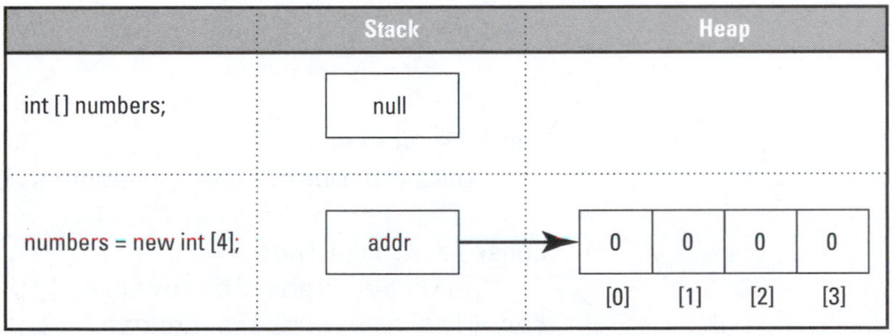

Figure 2-4

Internal representation of an array data structure

	Stack	Heap			
int [] numbers;	null				
numbers = new int [4];	addr →	0	0	0	0
		[0]	[1]	[2]	[3]

The variable `numbers` acts as a reference to the memory location assigned to the array. The array name can be used to access each array item directly. Remember that in the .NET Framework, all arrays are zero-based. That is, the first item of the array is accessed using an index of `0`, as follows:

```
numbers[0]
```

The second item is accessed by `numbers[1]`, and so on.

To work with an array, you first allocate the memory by creating and initializing an array as shown previously. Once the array is allocated, you can access any array element in whatever order that you please by directly referring to its index. For example, the following code assigns a value of 10 to the fourth item of the array and double of that value is then assigned to the variable `calc`:

```
numbers[3] = 10;
int calc = numbers[3] * 2;
```

The contents of an array are laid-out as a contiguous block of memory and can be directly accessed by using the array index. Therefore, reading from or writing to an array is extremely fast. However, arrays are limited by the requirements of homogeneity and fixed-size. Although array size can be increased, doing so requires reallocation of all the array elements and is a time-consuming operation. When an array stores data in a linear fashion as shown in Figure 2-4 and is accessed using a single index, it is called a single-dimensional array. This is in contrast with the multi-dimensional array such as a two-dimensional array where data is stored in a tabular fashion and can be referenced by a row index and a column index.

USE SINGLE-DIMENSIONAL ARRAYS

GET READY. To learn how to work with an array, perform the following steps:

1. Add a new C# Console Application project to the Lesson02 solution. Name the project as SingleDimensionalArray.

2. Replace the code in the Program file with the following code:

```csharp
using System;
using System.Linq;

namespace SingleDimensionalArrays
{
    class Program
    {
        static void Main(string[] args)
        {
            int[] numbers =
                new int[4] { 11, 7, 50, 45 };

            Console.WriteLine("Array items:");
            foreach (var item in numbers)
            {
                Console.WriteLine(item);
            }

            Console.WriteLine(
                "\nMax number: {0}", numbers.Max());

            Console.WriteLine(
                "\nArray items in reverse:");
            for (int i = numbers.Length - 1;
                    i >= 0; i--)
            {
                Console.WriteLine(numbers[i]);
            }
        }
    }
}
```

3. Run the project. A console window displays the output as shown in Figure 2-5.

Figure 2-5

Working with a single-dimensional array

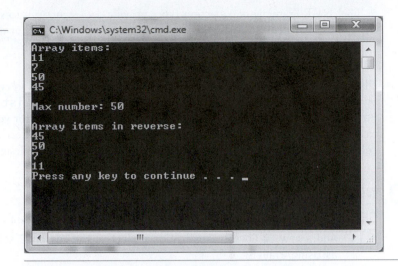

Understanding Multi-Dimensional Arrays

It is also possible to have multi-dimensional arrays. A *two-dimensional array* can be thought of as a table in which each cell is an array element and can be addressed by using the row number and the column number to which it belongs. Both the row number and column number are indexed by zero.

The following is an example of how a two-dimensional array is declared and initialized:

```
int[,] numbers = new int[3, 4]
{
    { 11, 7, 50, 45 },
    { 18, 35, 47, 24 },
    { 89, 67, 84, 34 },
};
```

TAKE NOTE*

An array can have a maximum of 32 dimensions.

This array is equivalent to creating a table with 3 rows and 4 columns. The expression `numbers[2, 3]` refers to an item at the third row and fourth column of an array by the name `numbers`, which in this case is 34. (Remember that the arrays are zero-based. Therefore a row index 2 represents the third row and the column index of 3 represents the fourth column).

The `Length` property for a multi-dimensional array returns the total count of all the items in the array. The `GetLength` method returns the number of size of a given dimension (where dimension is specified as a zero-based index). The two-dimensional array shown above, numbers, has a total of 12 items. It's first dimension is of size 3 and the second dimension is of the size 4:

```
Console.WriteLine(numbers.Length);         // 12

Console.WriteLine(numbers.GetLength(0));   // 3

Console.WriteLine(numbers.GetLength(1));   // 4
```

Using Collection Classes

The .NET Framework collection types provide data structures to store and manipulate a collection of items. These collection classes are defined as part of the System.Collections or System.Collections.Generic namespace.

The .NET Framework class libraries provide a variety of collection types as part of the System.Collections namespace. Some of these classes are ArrayList, Queue, Stack, and Hashtable. To make sure you choose the right collection type for your needs, it is important to understand the usage patterns that are expected from your collection. For example, some collections provide faster removal and insertions while some are designed for faster lookups.

⊙ WORK WITH ARRAYLIST

GET READY. To learn how to work with ArrayList, perform the following steps:

1. Add a new C# Console Application project to the Lesson02 solution. Name the project as UsingArrayList.

2. Replace the code in the Program file with the following code:

```
using System;
using System.Collections;
namespace UsingArrayList
{
    class Program
    {
        static void Main(string[] args)
        {
            ArrayList list = new ArrayList();
            list.Add("Monday");
            list.Add("Tuesday");
            list.Add("Wednesday");
            list.Add("Thursday");
            list.Add("Friday");
            list.Add("Saturday");
            list.Add("Sunday");

            Console.WriteLine("Original list:");
            foreach (var item in list)
            {
                Console.WriteLine(item);
            }
            list.Sort();
            Console.WriteLine("\nSorted list:");
            foreach (var item in list)
            {
                Console.WriteLine(item);
            }

            Console.WriteLine("\nItem Count: {0}",
                list.Count);
        }
    }
}
```

3. Run the project. A console window displays the output as shown in Figure 2-6.

Figure 2-6

Working with `ArrayList`

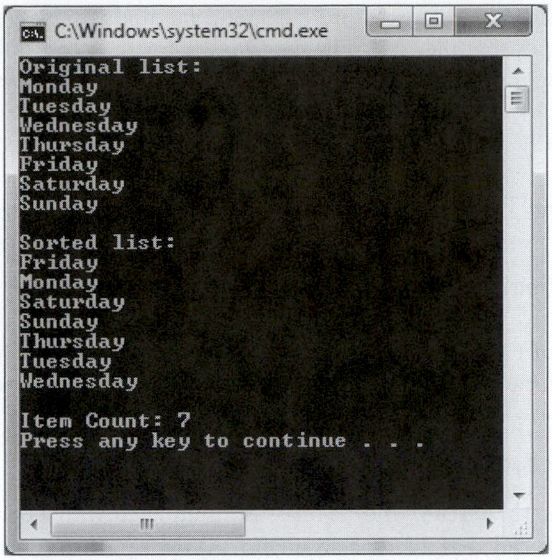

These collection classes get around an array's limitation of homogeneity and fixed size. The collections can dynamically expand at runtime when items are added. Also, these collections store their items as System.Object references, so they can store anything, as shown in the following code:

```
ArrayList list = new ArrayList();
list.Add("Hello");
list.Add(10);
list.Add(3.141);
list.Add(new int[] {1, 2, 3});

string itemString = (string) list[0];
int itemInt = (int) list[1];
double itemDouble = (double)list[2];
int[] itemIntArray = (int []) list[3];
```

The fact that these collections store items as System.Object causes two major issues:

- The first issue is the lack of type safety. Because you can store pretty much anything into a collection, you must rely on proper conversion and casting to make sure that you are retrieving the correct values. It is hard to enforce these checks at compile time and incorrect conversion and casting often leads to runtime errors that are difficult to debug.
- The second issue is the lack of performance, especially when dealing with value types. Because the collection stores object references, the values need to be boxed before they can be stored in a collection and unboxed when accessed. As previously discussed, each boxing and unboxing operation involves additional overhead, which can multiply by the number of items in the collections.

The .NET Framework introduced generic collections as part of .NET Framework 2.0; generic collections provide a type-safe alternative to the non-generic collection classes. By using the generic collection, you can avoid the issues of type safety and the boxing and unboxing performance issue. When using the .NET Framework 2.0 or later, you should only use a generic collection. The generic collections are part of the System.Collections.Generics namespace.

■ Understanding Generics

↓
THE BOTTOM LINE

The Generics feature helps you define classes that can be customized for different data types. Generics provide many benefits, including reusability, type-safety, and performance. The most common use of generics is to create collection classes.

Generics are classes, structures, interfaces, and methods that have placeholders for one or more of the types that they use. The placeholder for the type is also known as a type parameter. The following code illustrates a simple definition of a generic class.

```
public class DataStore<T>
{
        public T Id;
}
```

In this class definition, the letter T is used as the type parameter for the class definition. You can use any descriptive name here, but using the letter T is a common convention for defining generic types. You don't have to specify the actual data type corresponding to the type parameter until you create an instance of the class. The following code shows how to instantiate a generic class.

```
DataStore<int> productionData = new DataStore<int>();
productionData.Id = 10;
```

In this example, the `DataStore<T>` class is instantiated with a concrete type `int`. The concrete data type is also called as the type argument. At the run time, every occurrence of type parameter T is replaced with the specified type argument, which is `int` in this case. It's important to note that once a variable has been instantiated, its data type is fixed and cannot be changed.

You can use the same generic type to create yet another instance of the type `DataStore`, but this time passing a different type argument:

```
DataStore<string> employeeData =
                        new DataStore<string>();
employeeData.Id = "JOHNC";
```

Both `productionData` and `employeeData` variables are instances of the generic type `DataStore`. However by the virtue of a generic type, `productionData` has an integer member while `employeeData` has a string member.

Generic types are allowed to have more than one type parameters:

```
public class DataStore<TKey, TVal>
{
        public TKey Id;
        public TVal Value;
}
```

In this code, you specify the type parameters `TKey` and `TVal`, each of which will be replaced by the concrete data types specified by the type arguments when an instance of this class is created (as shown in the following code):

```
DataStore<int, string> myData =
        new DataStore<int, string>();

myData.Id = 10;

myData.Value = "Employee1";
```

Here, `TKey` gets replaced with the `int` data type whereas `TVal` gets replaced with the `string` data type. There is nothing special about the parameter names `TKey` and `TVal` and you are free to use a different name if you would like.

Understanding Constraints and Verifiability

Constraints specify restrictions to the kinds of types that client code can use for type arguments when it instantiates your class. *Verifiability* in context with generics refers to process of checking constraints to make sure that the code is memory safe.

In the previous code samples, you were able to instantiate a generic type with any type argument that you like. In some cases, you might want to have a control over the type arguments that may be used to instantiate a generic class. Say that you only support operations with the `string` data type or with an `Employee` class that you have defined elsewhere. You can put these restrictions in place by using constraints. Once you have put constraints in place, if the client code attempts to instantiate a class with a type that is not allowed by the constraint, the result is a compile-time error.

Constraints are specified using the `where` keyword. For example, consider the following class definition:

```
public class EmployeeRecord<T> where T : Employee
{
    public T employee;
}
```

This declaration ensures that when an instance of `EmployeeRecord` is created, the only valid type arguments are of the type `Employee` or one of classes derived from the `Employee` class. Once the compiler has this guarantee, it can allow methods and properties specific to the `Employee` class to be used in the `EmployeeRecord` class.

// Valid – type arguments satisfy the constraints

```
EmployeeRecord <Employee> employeeData =
                      new EmployeeRecord <Employee>();
```

// Invalid – generates compile-time error

```
EmployeeRecord <string> employeeData =
                      new EmployeeRecord <string>();
```

Constraints are used to make the generic code more reliable and less error-prone by specifying the types that will be supported.

When the code is compiled, the .NET Framework language compiler, such as the C# compiler, checks the code for verifiability. Verifiability is the process of making sure that the program is memory safe. *Memory safety* means that the program is only writing to or reading from the memory location it is intended too. For example, if a memory location stores a string value but the program tries to read that as an `Employee` value, unintended results could take place. By verifying that the program is memory safe, the compiler can help in eliminating such errors. In context of generics, verifiability can be checked by making sure that the constraints are checked each time when a class instance is created, a field is accessed, a method is invoked, and so on.

Understanding Contravariant and Covariance

Covarianvce is the ability to convert from less derived types to more derived types. *Contravariance*, on the other hand, is the ability to convert from more derived types to less derived types.

Covariance and contravariance of generic type parameters enable you to create instances of generic types whose type arguments are more derived (covariance) or less derived (contravariance) than what was specified in the definition of the generic type.

Covariance and contravariance are collectively referred to as variance. In contrast, a generic type parameter that is not marked covariant or contravariant is referred to as invariant. In the .NET Framework version 4, variant type parameters are restricted to generic interface and generic delegate types.

The following example illustrates covariant type parameters. In this example, there are two classes. The Person class has a Print method that takes an IEnumerable<Person> argument and prints the items in the sequence. The Employee class inherits from the Person class.

```
using System;
using System.Collections.Generic;

class Person
{
    public string Name { get; set; }

    public static void Print(
       IEnumerable<Person> persons)
    {
        foreach (var item in persons)
        {
            Console.WriteLine(item.Name);
        }
    }
}

class Employee : Person
{
    static void Main(string[] args)
    {
        List<Employee> employeeList =
          new List<Employee>();
        employeeList.Add(
          new Employee { Name = "John Doe" });

        Employee.Print(employeeList);

        IEnumerable<Person> emp = employeeList;
    }
}
```

The code in the Employee class creates a list with one item and demonstrates how an List<Employee> object can be passed to the Print method and assigned to a variable of type IEnumerable<Person> without casting.

The List<T> class implements IEnumerable<T>, which has a single covariant type parameter. The covariant type parameter is the reason why an instance of IEnumerable<Employee> can be used instead of IEnumerable<Person>.

The following example illustrates contravariant type parameters. The example defines a Person class with a DailyRate property. The example also defines a PersonDailyRateComparer class that implements IComparer<Person>. The implementation of the IComparer<T>.Compare method is based on the value of the DailyRate property, so PersonDailyRateComparer can be used to sort the Person objects by their daily rate.

```
using System;

using System.Collections.Generic;

class Person
{
    public virtual double DailyRate { get { return 0; } }
}
```

```csharp
class Employee : Person
{
    private double rate;
    private double hoursPerDay;
    public Employee (double rate, double hoursPerDay)
    {
        this.rate = rate;
        this.hoursPerDay = hoursPerDay;
    }


    public override double DailyRate
    {
        get
        {
            return rate * hoursPerDay;
        }
    }
}

class PersonDailyRateComparer : IComparer<Person>
{
    public int Compare(Person x, Person y)
    {
        if (x == null) return y == null ? 0 : -1;
        return y == null ? 1 : x.DailyRate.CompareTo
(y.DailyRate);
    }
}

class Program
{
    static void Main(string[] args)
    {
        SortedSet<Employee> employeesByDailyRate =
            new SortedSet<Employee>(new
PersonDailyRateComparer())
            {
                new Employee(40, 8),
                new Employee(35, 8),
                new Employee(50, 4)
            };

        foreach (var item in employeesByDailyRate)
        {
            Console.WriteLine(item.DailyRate);
        }
    }
}
```

The Employee class inherits Person and overrides the DailyRate property. The example creates a SortedSet<T> of Employee objects that uses PersonDailyRateComparer. This example can pass a comparer of a less derived type (Person) when the code calls for a more derived type (Employee), because the type parameter of the IComparer<T> generic interface is contravariant.

Understanding Generic Collections

Generic collections are more efficient and type-safe than their non-generic counter-parts from earlier versions of the .NET Framework. The .NET class library provides several ready-to-use generic collection classes as part of the System.Collections.Generic namespace.

CERTIFICATION READY
What is a generic collection?
2.6

A *generic collection* is a collection that stores only the items of the same data type. For example, you can have a list of integers in which all items are integer or you can have a list where all items are of the string data type. These generic collections solve the problems of type safety and performance associated with the non-generic collections.

To ensure type safety, the compiler ensures that you can only assign a value of the correct data type to each item in a generic collection. That is, if you define a list of integers, you can only store integers in that list. As a result, no casting or conversion operations are needed when retrieving and assigning values to such a list.

The generic collection types generally perform better than their non-generic equivalent. This is especially true in the case when the collection items are value types because with generics there is no need to box and unbox these items.

Generic collections are expressed using a special notation. For example, List<T> is a generic List collection. The T in the notation must be replaced with the data type that you want to store in the collection. The following are examples of how a generic List collection is defined and used:

```
List<int> listA; // defines an integer collection
listA.Add(10); // adds an integer to the list
listA.Add("Hello"); //compile-time error

List<string> listB; // defines a string collection
listB.Add("Hello"); // adds a string to the list
listB.Add(10); //compile-time error
```

Here, listA is a generic list that stores a collection of integers and listB is a generic list that stores a collection of string items.

Because the generic collections provide better performance and type safety, you should prefer to use a generic collection instead of a similar non-generic collection. Table 2-2 compares some generic collections with their non-generic equivalent.

Some collection classes such as LinkedList<T>, SortedDictionary<TKey, TValue> and KeyedCollection<TKey, TValue> are available only as generic collections.

The following exercise demonstrates how to work with the generic List class and use many of its properties.

Using List<T>

The List<T> class represents a generic list of a specified type. To create a list of integers, you say:

```
List<int> numbers = new List<int>();
```

Table 2-2

The generic and non-generic data types

NON-GENERIC COLLECTION	GENERIC COLLECTION	DESCRIPTION
ArrayList	List<T>	List<T> is a strongly-type collection of items. Most commonly used as a general-purpose collection.
Hashtable	Dictionary<TKey, TValue>	Dictionary<TKey, TValue> is used as a strongly-type dictionary where you can put a value and its associated key. TKey specifies the data type of the keys in the dictionary and TValue specifies the data type of the values in the dictionary. This data type is often used for lookups because retrieving a value by using its key is very fast.
Queue	Queue<T>	Queue<T> is a first-in, first-out (FIFO) data structure. That is, items added to the queue first will be processed first. Queue<T> is very useful for sequentially processing items as they arrive.
Stack	Stack<T>	Stack<T> is a last-in, first-out (LIFO) data structure. That is, items added to the stack last will be processed first. Stack<T> has many applications in programming and computer science.
SortedList	SortedList<TKey, TValue>	SortedList<TKey, TValue> is a collection of key/value pairs that are sorted by the key and can be accessed both by the key and the index. SortedList <TKey, TValue> provides very fast retrieval of data.
	LinkedList<T>	Provides a set of data items where each item contains a link to the memory location of the next and previous items. This collection is especially useful when the data items are not stored in contiguous memory locations.
	SortedDictionary <TKey, TValue>	This class is similar to SortedList class but is implemented as a dictionary. This class provides faster insertion and deletion than SortedList. The SortedList class takes less memory and provides faster retrieval.
	KeyedCollection <TKey, TValue>	This class is an abstract class that serves as a base class for creating collections where the key is the part of the value. For example if you are storing an Employee object as value then Employee.Id serves as the key. This class is useful for very fast retrieval.

Table 2-3 summarize some important methods and properties of the List class that are frequently used.

Table 2-3

Select members of the List<T> class

MEMBER	DESCRIPTION
Add	Add an item to the list. The following code adds the number 2 to the numbers list: `numbers.Add(2);`
AddRange	Adds a collection of items to a list. The following code add three integers to the numbers list: `Numbers.AddRange(new[] { 4, 8, 10 });`
Contains	Finds if the given item is present in the list. The following code returns True if the number 2 exists in the list: `numbers.Contains(2);`

Insert	Inserts the given item at the specified index. The following code inserts the number 6 at the (zero-based) index 2.
	`//before: {2, 4, 8, 10}`
	`numbers.Index(2, 6);`
	`//after: {2, 4, 6, 8, 10}`

Count	Return the number of items in the list. If the list contains {2, 4, 6, 8, 10}, the expression, numbers.Count, returns a value of 5.

 WORK WITH A GENERIC LIST COLLECTION

GET READY. Perform the following steps to work with the generic List collection.

1. Create a new C# Console Application project. Name the project as GenericList.

2. Modify the code for the Main method in the Program file with the following code:

```
static void Main(string[] args)
{
    List<int> numbers = new List<int>();
    // add items to the list
    numbers.Add(2);
    numbers.AddRange(new[] { 4, 8, 10 });

    Console.WriteLine("Number of items: {0}",
        numbers.Count);
    // iterate through the list items
    foreach (var item in numbers)
    {
        Console.WriteLine(item);
    }
    Console.WriteLine("List contains the number 6? {0}",
        numbers.Contains(6));
    numbers.Insert(2, 6);

    Console.WriteLine("Number of items: {0}",
        numbers.Count);
```

```
        Console.WriteLine("Item at index [2]: {0}",
            numbers[2]);
        foreach (var item in numbers)
        {
            Console.WriteLine(item);
        }
    }
}
```

3. Run the project. A console window displays the output from the program as shown in Figure 2-7.

Figure 2-7

Working with `Generic List`

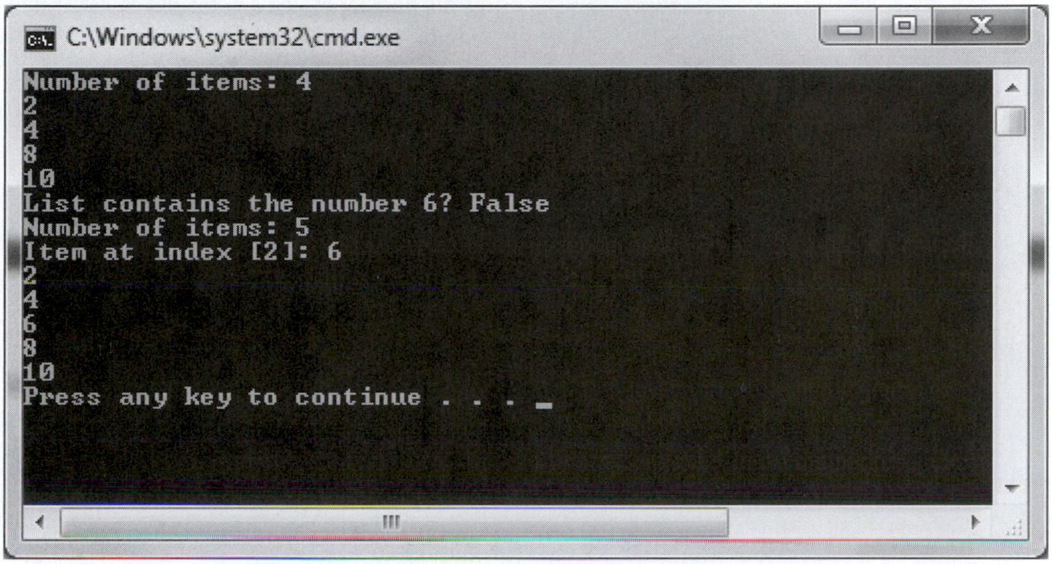

```
C:\Windows\system32\cmd.exe

Number of items: 4
2
4
8
10
List contains the number 6? False
Number of items: 5
Item at index [2]: 6
2
4
6
8
10
Press any key to continue . . . _
```

The previous exercise creates a generic List collection for storing integers and demonstrates how to add and insert items to the list. The exercise also shows how to use other properties and methods of the `List<T>` class, such as `Count`, `add`, `addrange`, `insert`, and `Contains`.

Using LinkedList<T>

The LinkedList<T> class represents a collection where each item contains a link to the memory location of the next and previous items. The items in a linked list are not stored in contiguous memory location. The links stored with each item is used to traverse back and forth across the list. A linked list is very effective for storing data that will have frequent insertions and deletions.

The following code creates an object for storing a linked list of strings:

```
string[] words = {
    "Konbu", "Tofu",
    "Pavlova", "Chocolate",
    "Ikura" };
LinkedList<string> list =
    new LinkedList<string>(words);
```

The following table summarizes some important methods and properties of the LinkedList<T> class.

Table 2-4

Select members of the
LinkedList<T> class

MEMBER	DESCRIPTION
AddFirst	Add an item to the beginning of a linked list. The following code adds the string "Chai" to the beginning of the list: `list.AddFirst("Chai");`
AddLast	Add an item to the end of a linked list. The following code adds the string "Chai" to the end of the list: `list.AddLast("Chai");`
Count	Gets the number of items in the linked list. If the linked list, list, contains {"Konbu", "Tofu", "Pavlova", "Chocolate", "Ikura"}, the expression `list.Count` returns a value of 5.
Contains	Finds if the given item is present in the list. The following code returns *True* if the string "Tofu" exists in the list: `list.Contains("Tofu");`

Using Queue<T>

Queue<T> is a first-in, first-out (FIFO) data structure. That is, items added to the queue first will be processed first. Queue<T> is very useful for sequentially processing items as they arrive. For example, a print spooler may use a queue for storing the print jobs and process them as they arrive.

To create a queue of integers, you say:

```
Queue<int> jobQueue = new Queue<int>();
```

The following table summarizes some important methods and properties of the Queue<T> class that are frequently used.

Table 2-5

Select members of the
Queue<T> class

MEMBER	DESCRIPTION

Enqueue	Adds an item to the end of the queue. The following code adds the number 2 and 4 to a queue named jobQueue. The number 2 is added first followed by number 4, 8 and finally 10.
	
	`jobQueue.Enqueue(2);`
	
	`jobQueue.Enqueue(4);`
	
	`jobQueue.Enqueue(8);`
	
	`jobQueue.Enqueue(10);`

Dequeue	Removes an item from the beginning of the queue and returns it:
	
	The following code returns the value of 2 because that was the first item to be added to the queue.
	
	`//before: {2, 4, 8, 10}`
	
	`jobQueue.Dequeue(); //returns 2`
	
	`//after: {4, 8, 10}`

(continued)

MEMBER	DESCRIPTION
Contains	Determines if the given item is present in the queue.

Peek	Returns the item at the beginning of the queue without removing it.
	`//before: {2, 4, 8, 10}`
	`jobQueue.Peek(); //returns 2`
	`//after: {2, 4, 8, 10}`

Count	Return the number of items in the queue.

Using Stack<T>

Stack<T> is a last-in, first-out (LIFO) data structure. That is, items added to the stack last will be processed first. Stack<T> has many applications in programming and computer science such as program execution and expression evaluation.

To create a stack of integers, you say:

```
Stack<int> expressionStack = new Stack<int>();
```

The following table summarizes some important methods and properties of the Stack<T> class that are frequently used.

Table 2-6

Select members of the Stack<T> class

MEMBER	DESCRIPTION

Push	Adds an item to the top of the stack. The following code adds the number 2 and 4 to a stack named expressionStack. After the operations complete, the number 10 is at the top of the stack.
	`expressionStack.Push(2);`
	`expressionStack.Push(4);`
	`expressionStack.Push(8);`
	`expressionStack.Push(10);`

Pop	Removes an item from the top of the stack and returns it:
	The following code returns the value of 10 because that was the last item to be added to the stack
	`//before: {2, 4, 8, 10}`
	`expressionStack.Pop(); //returns 10`
	`//after: {2, 4, 8}`

Contains	Determines if the given item is present on the stack.

Peek	Returns the item at the top of the stack without removing it.
	`//before: {2, 4, 8, 10}`
	`expressionStack.Peek(); //returns 10`
	`//after: {2, 4, 8, 10}`

Count	Return the number of items on the stack.

SKILL SUMMARY

IN THIS LESSON YOU LEARNED:

- Data types specify the kind of data that you work with in a program. The data type defines the size of memory needed to store the data and the kind of operation that can be performed on the data.
- Intrinsic data types are the primitive data types for which the support is directly built into the programming language.
- The value types directly store the value whereas the reference types store only a reference to the actual value.
- The data types specify rules for converting values in one type to another type. The conversion can be performed implicitly by the compiler or explicitly by using the cast operator. Not all data type conversions are permissible; when a conversion is not permitted, an `InvalidCastException` is thrown by the runtime.
- Boxing is the process of converting a value type to the reference type. Unboxing is the process of converting a reference type to the value type.
- An array is a collection of items stored in a contiguous memory location. Each item of an array can be accessed by using a unique index.
- The .NET Framework collection types provide data structures to store and manipulate a collection of items. These collection classes are defined as part of the System.Collections or System.Collections.Generic namespace.
- The generic collections are more efficient and type-safe than their non-generic counterparts from the earlier versions of the .NET Framework. The .NET class library provides several ready to use generic collection classes as part of the System.Collections.Generic namespace.

■ Knowledge Assessment

Fill in the Blank

Complete the following sentences by writing the correct word or words in the blanks provided.

1. _____ are the primitive data types for which the support is directly built into the programming language.

2. To access the first element of an array, use an index of _____.

3. In the C# programming language, the data types for variables, constants, method return values, and parameters must be known at _____.

4. The reference types store only a _____ to a memory location that contains the actual data.

5. _____ is the process of converting a value type to the reference type. _____ is the process of converting an reference type to the value type.

6. An array is a collection of items, of the same data type, stored in a _____ memory location and addressed by using the array's _____.

7. The memory allocated in the _____ is automatically reclaimed by the garbage collector when the objects are not in use anymore.

8. _____ is the generic class that corresponds to `ArrayList`.

9. _____ ensures that you can only assign a value of the correct data type to a generic collection.

10. The generic collection classes are defined as part of the _____ namespace.

Multiple Choice

Circle the letter that corresponds to the best answer.

1. You need to store values ranging from 0 to 255. You need to also make sure that your program minimizes memory use. Which data type should you use to store these values?
   a. byte
   b. char
   c. short
   d. int

2. You write the following code snippet:

```
int[] numbers = {1, 2, 3, 4};
int val = numbers[1];
```

   What is the value of the variable val after this code snippet is executed?
   a. 1
   b. 2
   c. 3
   d. 4

3. You need to create a variable that stores multiple unicode characters. Which data type should you use to define such a variable?
   a. byte
   b. sbyte
   c. char
   d. string

4. You need to create a structured data type named Point. Point should have two fields (X and Y), each of the float data type. Programs that use the Point data type should be able to directly reference the fields X and Y. You need to make sure that Point is a value data type so that the value of the variable is directly stored in its assigned memory location. How should you define such a data type?
   a.
```
public class Point
{
    private int X, Y;
}
```
   b.
```
public class Point
{
    public int X, Y;
}
```
   c.
```
public struct Point
{
    private int X, Y;
}
```
   d.
```
public struct Point
{
    public int X, Y;
}
```

5. Which of the following statements, when executed, will throw an exception of the type `InvalidCastException`?

   a.
   ```
   int number1 = 12;
   double number2 = number1;
   ```
   b.
   ```
   double number2 = 3.141;
   int number1 = number2;
   ```
   c.
   ```
   int i = 10;
   object o = i;
   ```
   d.
   ```
   object o = 10;
   int i = (int) o;
   ```

6. You write the following code in your program:

   ```
   double p = 3.141;
   object o = p;
   int i = (int) o;
   ```

   Not all data type conversion is permissible. When you run this code, which of the following exceptions should you expect to receive?
   a. `System.InvalidCastException`
   b. `System.InvalidOperationException`
   c. `System.InvalidDataException`
   d. `System.FormatException`

7. You are using a HashTable collection in your program. You want to modify your program to take advantage of type safety and increased performance offered by the generic types. Which of the following generic types should you use to replace HashTable with in your program?
   a. `Collection<T>`
   b. `Dictionary<TKey, TValue>`
   c. `List<T>`
   d. `SortedList<TKey, TValue>`

8. You are working with the `List<T>` collection in a program that you are developing. You write the following code:

   ```
   List<int> numbers = new List<int>();
   numbers.AddRange(new[] { 2, 6, 8 });
   ```

   You need to insert the number 4 between the number 2 and 6. What code should you write to accomplish this?
   a. `numbers.Insert(4, 1);`
   b. `numbers.Insert(1, 4);`
   c. `numbers.Insert(2, 4);`
   d. `numbers.Insert(4, 2);`

9. You are developing a C# program. The program declares a variable that represents the first-in, first-out collection of values of the double data type. You need to make sure that you are not able to store any other data type in the collection. What data type should you use to declare the variable in your program?
   a. Queue
   b. Queue<double>
   c. Stack
   d. Stack<double>

10. You are developing a C# program. The program declares a variable that represents a strongly typed collection of values of the double data type. The values of the collection can only be manipulated in the order of last-in, first-out. Which data type should you use to declare the variable in your program?
    a. Queue
    b. Queue<double>
    c. Stack
    d. Stack<double>

■ Competency Assessment

Project 2-1: Using Two-dimensional Arrays

You are writing a program that uses a two-dimensional array. The array has 4 rows and 5 columns. You need to print the largest element in each row of the array.

Project 2-2: Using a Linked List

You are writing a program that stores the list of product names in a linked list. The user will enter a product name and your program needs to check if the linked list contains the given product. How would you write such a program?

■ Proficiency Assessment

Project 2-3: Using a Generic Queue Collection

You are writing a program that uses two queues. The data in each queue is already in the ascending order. You need to process the contents of both the queues in such a way that the output is printed on the screen in sorted order. You should be using to the generic version of the Queue class to benefit from type safety and faster performance. How should you write a program to address this scenario?

Project 2-4: Using a Generic Stack Collection

You are writing a program that uses two stacks. The data in each stack is already in the descending order. You need to process the contents of both the stacks in such a way that the output is printed on the screen in the ascending order. You should be using to the generic version of the Stack class to benefit from type safety and faster performance. How should you write a program to address this scenario?

Understanding Events and Exceptions

EXAM OBJECTIVE MATRIX

SKILLS/CONCEPTS	MTA EXAM OBJECTIVE	MTA EXAM OBJECTIVE NUMBER
Understanding Events and Event Handling in the .NET Framework	Understand events and event handling in the .NET Framework.	1.2
Understanding Structured Exception Handling in the .NET Framework	Understand structured exception handling in the .NET Framework.	1.3
Understanding Basic Application Settings	Understand basic application settings.	1.1

KEY TERMS

app.config

application settings

delegate

event

exception

web.config

You are a software developer for the Northwind Corporation. As part of your job, you develop computer programs to solve business problems. You write programs that are interactive and can respond to events generated by the user interface and business processes.

It is important for you to make sure that while you design your programs as per the specifications, your programs are able to recover from the faults that are not part of normal processing. The programs that you write need to be robust and should be able to display error message but continue processing.

Your programs should also provide flexibility so that you can change certain settings at runtime without the need to modify the source code.

Understanding Events and Event Handling in the .NET Framework

↓ THE BOTTOM LINE

An *event* enables an object to notify other objects or classes when something of interest occurs. Event-driven programming is a popular way to create user-interface based applications (such as Windows and Web applications) where you write methods that respond to events raised by controls such as buttons and list controls.

CERTIFICATION READY
How does event handling work in the .NET Framework?
1.2

Creating Delegates

A *delegate* is a special type that can hold a reference to a method. Delegates are commonly used to provide event-handling functionality.

A delegate is a reference type, but unlike other reference types, it holds a reference to a method rather than an object. You create a delegate with the `delegate` keyword, followed by a return type, the name of the new delegate, and the signature of the method that the delegate can reference to, as follows.

```
public delegate void MyDelegate
    (string param1, string param2);
```

This declaration defines a delegate named `MyDelegate`, which can hold reference to any method that returns nothing and accepts two string parameters, such as the following method:

```
void Method1 (string param1,string param2)
{
    return;
}
```

The `delegate` type can be used to declare a variable that can refer to a method with the same signature as the delegate. For example, you can say:

```
MyDelegate handler;
handler += Method1;
```

At this point, the `handler` variable is a delegate with a reference to the `Method1`. Notice that the syntax uses the addition assignment operation. It means that you can associate more than one method (of compatible signature) with the delegate object, creating an invocation list of one or more methods.

You can indirectly call the `Method1` in this example by using the `handler` delegate:

```
handler("string1", "string2");
```

When the delegate is called like this, it invokes all the methods in its invocation list. In this specific example, the handler object refers to only one method (`Method1`) and, therefore, `Method1` will be invoked with the two string objects as parameters.

Among many other applications, the delegates form the basis for event declarations, as discussed in the next section.

Defining Events

> Events are a way for an object to notify other classes or objects when something of interest happens. The object that sends the notification is called as a publisher of the event. The object or class that receives the notification is called the subscriber of the event.

Events are easy to understand in the context of graphical user interfaces (GUI). When a user clicks a button, a *Click* event occurs on the button control. When a user moves the mouse over an image control, a *MouseMove* event occurs. When a user pushes the mouse button down, a *MouseDown* event takes place. These are just some of the examples of events. Most classes in the .NET Framework class libraries define their own events. You can find the events defined by a class by looking at the documentation for a given class. Multiple user interface elements can subscribe to this event and change their visual state accordingly (for example, some controls get enabled or disabled). In this type of event communication, the event publishers do not need to know which objects subscribe to the events that are being raised.

Events are not just limited to GUI programming. In fact, events play an important role in the .NET Framework class libraries as a way for objects to publish any change in their state, such as the arrival of an email message, a modification to a file, changes in time, the completion of a process, and so on. You'll work with events in practically all programs.

An event can have multiple subscribers, and each subscriber can respond differently to an event. When an event occurs, the publisher of the event might not necessarily know which method will handle that event. The .NET Framework provides a mechanism for connecting the event publisher and subscriber through special delegate types.

Events are based on delegates. The delegate corresponding to an event can specify the signature of the methods that can receive notification for the event.

When you define events, you generally need two pieces of information:

- A class that contains the event data. This class is usually derived from the **EventArgs** class.
- A delegate that connects the event with its handler method(s).

To define an event, you can use a custom delegate. But in most cases, if your event holds no event-specific data, using the predefined delegate (**EventHandler**) is sufficient. The **EventHandler** delegate is defined as follows:

```
public delegate void EventHandler(
        Object sender, EventArgs e);
```

Here, the sender parameter is a reference to the object that raises the event, and the **e** parameter is a reference to an event data object that contains no event data.

The **EventArgs** class is used by events that do not pass any event-related information to an event handler when an event is raised. If the event handler requires event-related information, the application must derive a class from the **EventArgs** class to hold the event-related data.

⊕ PUBLISH AND SUBSCRIBE TO EVENTS

GET READY. Before you begin these steps, be sure to launch Microsoft Visual Studio and open a new Console Application Project named Lesson01. Then perform the following steps:

1. Create a new project based on the Console Application template. Name the project as EventPubSub.
2. Add a new class file (Rectangle.cs) to the project. Modify the code of class Rectangle as follows:

```
class Rectangle
{
    // Declare an event named Changed of
    // delegate type EventHandler
    public event EventHandler Changed;
    private double length;
    public double Length
    {
        get
        {
            return length;
        }
        set
        {
            length 5 value;
            // Publish the Changed event
            Changed(this, EventArgs.Empty);
        }
    }
}
```

TAKE NOTE *

The EventArgs.Empty field represents an event with no event data. This field is equivalent to having a read-only instance of the EventArgs class.

3. Modify the code of the Program class as follows:

```
class Program
{
    static void Main(string[] args)
    {
        Rectangle rect = new Rectangle();
        // Subscribe to the Changed event
        rect.Changed += new EventHandler(Rectangle_Changed);
        rect.Length = 10;
    }

    static void Rectangle_Changed(object sender, EventArgs e)
    {
        Rectangle rect = (Rectangle)sender;
        Console.WriteLine(
            "Value Changed: Length = {0}",
            rect.Length);
    }
}
```

4. Click **Debug > Start Without Debugging**. A console window displays, indicating the value of the Length property is changed.

Here the Rectangle class defines a Changed event that is invoked when the Length property of the Rectangle object is changed. The delegate of the Changed event is of the EventHandler type. In the Rectangle class, the Changed event is invoked when the set accessor of the Length property is called.

You subscribe to the Changed event inside the Main method by attaching the Rectangle_ Changed method as an event handler for the event by using the following code:

```
rect.Changed += new EventHandler(Rectangle_Changed);
```

The signature of the Rectangle_Changed method matches the requirements of the EventHandler delegate. The Rectangle_Changed method is invoked as soon as you set the value of Length property in the Main method.

The above code uses the += operator rather than the simple assignment operator (=) for attaching the event handler. By using the += operator, you make sure that this event handler will be added to a list of event handlers already attached with the event. This technique allows you to have multiple event handlers that may respond to an event. For example, when a button is pressed, one event handler may print a document while the other event handler may end an email. At times, an event handler may be defined as part of a base class, so there might be event handlers attached to an object even if you don't see them in your code. If you use the assignment operator (=) to assign the new event handler, it will override any existing event handler that is attached to the event; the newly attached event handler will be the only one that will get fired when the event is invoked. In most cases, you should avoid using the assignment operator to assign a new event handler because you may accidentally remove an existing event handler (such as a event handler in the base class).

■ Understanding Structured Exception Handling in the .NET Framework

↓ THE BOTTOM LINE

The .NET Framework supports standard exception handling to raise and handle runtime errors. In this section, you'll learn how to use try, catch, and finally keywords to handle exceptions.

CERTIFICATION READY
How are exceptions handled in the .NET Framework?
1.3

An *exception* is an error condition that occurs during the execution of a .NET program. When this happens, the runtime creates an object to represent the error and "throws" it. Unless you "catch" the exception by writing proper exception handling code, the program execution will terminate.

For example, if you attempt to divide an integer by zero, a DivideByZeroException type exception will be thrown. In the .NET Framework, an exception is represented by using an object of the System.Exception or one of its derived classes. There are predefined exception classes that represent many commonly occurring error situations (such as the DivideByZeroException). If you are designing an application that needs to throw any application-specific exceptions, you should create a custom exception class that derives from the System.Exception class.

Handling Exceptions

To handle exceptions, place the code that throws exceptions inside a try block and place the code that handles the exceptions inside one or more catch blocks immediately below the try block.

The following exercise shows how to use a try-catch block to handle an exception. This exercise uses the File.OpenText method to open a disk file. This statement will execute just fine in the normal case, but if the file is missing, or the permission to read the file is missing, then an exception is thrown.

➔ HANDLE AN EXCEPTION

GET READY. To handle an exception, perform the following steps.

1. Create a new console application project named Exceptions.
2. Add the following using directive to the Program.cs file:

   ```
   using System.IO;
   ```

3. Add the following code to the Main method of the Program class:

   ```
   ExceptionTest();
   ```

4. Add the following method to the `Program.cs` class:

```
private static void ExceptionTest()
{
    StreamReader sr = null;
    try
    {
        sr = File.OpenText(@"c:\data.txt");
        Console.WriteLine(sr.ReadToEnd());
    }
    catch (FileNotFoundException fnfe)
    {
        Console.WriteLine(fnfe.Message);
    }
    catch(Exception ex)
    {
        Console.WriteLine(ex.Message);
    }
}
```

5. Create a text file ("data.txt") by using Notepad or Visual Studio on the c: drive. It is okay to create the file at a different location, but if you do so, remember to modify the file location in the program.

6. Write some text in the file.

7. Set the project as the startup project. Click **Debug > Start Without Debugging** or press **Ctrl+F5**.

8. You'll see that the contents of the text file are displayed in a command Window. Press a key to close the console window.

9. Delete the data.txt file and run the program again. This time, you'll get a `FileNotFoundException` error and a related message will be displayed in the output window.

TAKE NOTE＊ In the `ExceptionTest` method, don't change the order of the two catch blocks. The more specific exceptions need to be listed before the generic exceptions; otherwise, you'll get compilation error.

TAKE NOTE＊

A `try` block must have at least a `catch` block or a `finally` block associated with it.

To handle the exception, enclose the statements that could cause the exception in a `try` block. Then add `catch` blocks to handle one or more exceptions. In this example, in addition to handling the more specific `FileNotFoundException` exception, we are also using a `catch` block with `Exception` to catch all other exceptions. The exception type name for a catch block must be included inside the parenthesis along with the optional parameter name (to provide access to the exception object). The statements that are executed when an exception is caught must be included within a curly brace (}).

The code execution stops when an exception occurs. The runtime searches for an enclosing `try` block and then checks that block's catch list for a `catch` statement that matches with, or is a base class of, the type of exception. When the runtime finds a matching `catch` block, it executes it and then continues normal code execution. If the first `catch` block listed under the `try` block doesn't catch the raised exception, the control moves on to the next catch block, and so on. If the exception is not handled in the catch list, the runtime checks for the next `try` block and `catch` statements in the calling code and continues to do so for rest of the call stack. Upon reaching the end of the `call` stack, if no `catch` block has been found, the .NET runtime default behavior is to terminate the application.

Using try-catch-finally

The `finally` block is used in association with the `try` block. The `finally` block is always executed regardless of whether an exception is thrown. The `finally` block is often used to write clean-up code.

When the exception occurs, it often means that some lines of code after the exception occurred were not executed. This can often leave your program in a dirty or unstable state. You can use the `finally` statement to guarantee that certain cleanup code is always executed. This can involve closing connections, releasing resources, or setting up variables to their expected values. The `finally` block can immediately follow the `try` block if no exception handling other than `cleanup` is needed. More frequently, the `finally` block follows the last `catch` block so that exceptions can be handled as well. Let's look at the code in the following exercise:

USE TRY-CATCH-FINALLY

GET READY. To use `try-catch-finally`, perform the following steps:

1. Create a new console application project named TryCatchFinally.
2. Add the following `using` directive to the Program.cs file:

   ```
   using System.IO;
   ```

3. Add the following code to the `Main` method of the Program.cs class:

   ```
   TryCatchFinallyTest();
   ```

4. Add the following method to the Program.cs class:

   ```csharp
   private static void TryCatchFinallyTest()
   {
       StreamReader sr = null;
       try
       {
           sr = File.OpenText(@"c:\data.txt");
           Console.WriteLine(sr.ReadToEnd());
       }
       catch (FileNotFoundException fnfe)
       {
           Console.WriteLine(fnfe.Message);
       }
       catch (Exception ex)
       {
           Console.WriteLine(ex.Message);
       }
       finally
       {
           if (sr != null)
           {
               sr.Close();
           }
           Console.WriteLine("The finally block ran");
       }
   }
   ```

5. Create a text file ("data.txt") by using Notepad or Visual Studio on the c: drive. It is okay to create the file at a different location, but if you do so, remember to modify the file location in the program.

6. Write some text in the file.

7. Set the project as the startup project. Click **Debug > Start Without Debugging** or press **Ctrl+F5**.

8. You'll see that the contents of the text file are displayed in a command window. Press a key to close the console window.

9. Delete the data.txt file and run the program again. This time you'll get a `FileNotFoundException` error and an appropriate message will be displayed in the output window.

In this exercise, the program makes sure that the `StreamReader` object is closed and any resources are released when the operation completes. The code in the `finally` block is executed regardless of whether an exception is thrown or not.

Understanding Basic Application Settings

 THE BOTTOM LINE

Application settings allow the applications to store custom application-specific data. The settings data is stored as XML in a disk file. Application settings allow the programs to change certain settings at runtime without the need to modify the program's source code

Your application might need to provide settings that might change from installation to installation. For example, if your application connects to a database, you may want flexibility in specifying where the database is located. If you hard-code the database location at compile time, users will not have any flexibility to change the location at runtime. However you can use the .NET Framework application settings to store configurable settings and make your program more flexible at runtime.

Settings are specified in an XML-based settings file. You can change these settings after the application is compiled. When the application starts, it dynamically reads the settings data to change its behavior at the runtime.

The <configuration> element is the required root element in every configuration file. Each configuration file must contain exactly one root element.

The <configuration> element can further have other elements, such as <appSettings> and <connectionStrings>. The <appSettings> section contains custom application settings while <connectionStrings> specifies a collection of the database connection strings.

Both sections use add, remove, or clear tags to control the values being provided to the application.

For Web applications, you store the application settings in a file named web.config. For other applications, including console applications, Windows Forms applications, and Windows Presentation Foundation (WPF) applications, the application settings are specified in an app.config file.

Using App.Config

App.config is an XML-based configuration file that is used to change an application's behavior at runtime.

The app.config file is used to store any data that you do not want to include directly in the application code. Settings in the app.config file are stored as XML data. The app.config file can store both application-specific settings and user-specific settings.

The application-specific settings are represented by the `<appSettings>` element. When the application is compiled to an .exe file, the application-specific settings are stored in the app.exe config file where app.exe is the name of the application's executable file. When you deploy your application, you must deploy the app.exe config file with your application in the same folder as the application's executable file.

The following exercise shows you how to use application settings from the app.config file.

USE THE APP.CONFIG FILE

GET READY. To use application settings from the app.config file, perform the following steps:

1. Create a new console application project named AppConfig.
2. Click **Project > Add New Item** and then select the Application Configuration File template. Name the file app.config.
3. Add the following XML to the app.config file:

```xml
<?xml version="1.0" encoding="utf-8" ?>
<configuration>
    <appSettings>
        <add key="LogFile" value="c:\logs\App.log"/>
        <add key="AdminEmail" value="admin@microsoft.com"/>
    </appSettings>
    <connectionStrings>
        <add name="prodServer"
connectionString="server=ProdServer;database=northwind;
  Integrated Security=SSPI;Persist Security Info=False"/>
    </connectionStrings>
</configuration>
```

4. Modify the code for the Main method as follows:

```csharp
static void Main(string[] args)
{
    string logFile = ConfigurationManager.
        AppSettings["LogFile"];
    string adminEmail = ConfigurationManager.
        AppSettings["AdminEmail"];
    string connString = ConfigurationManager.
        ConnectionStrings["prodServer"].ConnectionString;
        Console.WriteLine("LogFile: {0}", logFile);
        Console.WriteLine("AdminEmail: {0}", adminEmail);
        Console.WriteLine("connection string: {0}",
          connString);
}
```

5. Click **Project > Add Reference.** The Add Reference dialog box displays.

6. On the .NET tab, click System.Configuration (see Figure 3-1).

Figure 3-1

Selecting System.Configuration

Component Name	Version	Runtime	Path
System.AddIn.Contract	4.0.0.0	v4.0.30319	C:\Prog
System.AddIn	4.0.0.0	v4.0.30319	C:\Prog
System.ComponentModel.Co...	4.0.0.0	v4.0.30319	C:\Prog
System.ComponentModel.Data...	4.0.0.0	v4.0.30319	C:\Prog
System.Configuration	4.0.0.0	v4.0.30319	C:\Prog
System.Configuration.Install	4.0.0.0	v4.0.30319	C:\Prog
System.Core	4.0.0.0	v4.0.30319	C:\Prog
System.Data.DataSetExtensions	4.0.0.0	v4.0.30319	C:\Prog
System.Data	4.0.0.0	v4.0.30319	C:\Prog
System.Data.Entity	4.0.0.0	v4.0.30319	C:\Prog

Add Reference

.NET | COM | Projects | Browse | Recent

Filtered to: .NET Framework 4 Client Profile

OK   Cancel

7. Add the following `using` directive to the code:

   ```
   using System.Configuration;
   ```

8. Build the project. You'll notice that an AppConfig.exe.config file is created in the project's output folder. This file, by default, contains the application settings specified in the app.config file.

9. Set the project as the startup project by clicking **Debug > Start Without Debugging** (or by pressing **Ctrl+F5**).

10. You'll see that the following messages are displayed in a command Window:

    ```
    LogFile: c:\logs\App.log
    AdminEmail: admin@microsoft.com
    connection string:
        server=ProdServer;database=northwind;Integrated Security=SSPI
    ;Persist Security Info=False
    ```

11. Close the command window. Directly modify the AppConfig.exe.config file and change the LogFile value to "d:\logs\newLog.log".

12. Run the AppConfig.exe without building the program. You'll notice that the modified value of LogFile is displayed in the console window.

In this exercise, you used the `ConfigurationManager` class to access the settings from the application configuration file. The `ConfigurationManager` class provides two properties. The `AppSettings` property gets the data from the `appSettings` section of the configuration file. The `ConnectionStrings` property gets the data from the `connectionStrings` section of the configuration file.

Using the Web.Config File

Web.config is the configuration file for any ASP.NET Web site or Web service. The web.config file is used to store the settings that you might need to modify after an application has been built.

The *web.config* file stores ASP.NET configuration data in an XML format. The web.config file allows you to edit the configuration data without any changes to the Web application's source code. You can use the web.config file to specify database connection strings, authentication modes, page caching, custom errors, many custom settings, and so on.

The web.config file allows you to configure a Web application at multiple levels. For example, you can have one web.config file at the application's level and you can also have additional web.config files in application subdirectories. A configuration setting specified in the child subdirectory overrides the same setting specified in the parent directory.

The root of the ASP.NET configuration hierarchy is the root web.config file located in the .NET Framework's config folder (usually at <systemroot>\Microsoft.NET\Framework\ <versionNumber>\CONFIG\Web.config). This web.config includes settings that apply to all ASP.NET applications that run a specific version of the .NET Framework. Each ASP.NET application inherits default configuration settings from the root web.config file, so in the application specific web.config files, you need to create only the settings that override the default settings specified in the root web.config file.

USE THE WEB.CONFIG FILE

GET READY. To use the web.config file, perform the following steps:

1. Create a new C# ASP.NET Empty Web Application project. Name the project as WebConfig.

2. Modify the XML for the web.config file as follows:

```
<?xml version="1.0"?>
<configuration>
  <appSettings>
    <add key="LogFile" value="c:\logs\App.log"/>
  </appSettings>
  <connectionStrings>
    <add name="prodServer" connectionString="server=ProdServer;
    database=northwind;Integrated Security=SSPI;Persist Security
    Info=False"/>
  </connectionStrings>
  <system.web>
    <compilation debug="true" targetFramework="4.0"/>
  </system.web>
</configuration>
```

3. Add a new Web Form (default.aspx) to the project.

   Open the code-behind file (default.aspx.cs) for the default.aspx page and modify the code for the Page_Load method as follows:

```
protected void Page_Load(object sender, EventArgs e)
{
        string logFile = WebConfigurationManager.
           AppSettings["LogFile"];
        Response.Write(String.Format(
        "<p>LogFile: {0}</p>", logFile));
```

```
            ConnectionStringSettings connString =
               WebConfigurationManager.
               ConnectionStrings["ProdServer"];
            Response.Write(String.Format(
               "<p>Connection String: {0}</p>",
               connString.ConnectionString));
         }
```

4. Add the following using directives to the code:

   ```
   using System.Configuration;
   using System.Web.Configuration;
   ```

5. Set the project as the startup project.

6. Build and run the project. You'll see the following messages displayed on the browser window.

   ```
   LogFile: c:\logs\App.log
   Connection String: server=ProdServer;database=northwind;
   Integrated Security=SSPI
   ;Persist Security Info=False
   ```

7. Do not close the browser window. Modify the web.config file and change the LogFile value to "d:\logs\newLog.log" and then save the file.

8. Refresh the browser. You'll notice that the modified value of LogFile is displayed in the browser.

   ```
   LogFile: d:\logs\newLog.log
   Connection String: server=ProdServer;database=northwind;
   Integrated Security=SSPI
   ;Persist Security Info=False
   ```

In this exercise, you used the WebConfigurationManager class to access the settings from the web configuration file. The WebConfigurationManager class is the preferred way to work with the configuration files related to Web applications. The WebConfigurationManager class provides two properties:

- The AppSettings property gets the data from the appSettings section of the configuration file.
- The ConnectionStrings property gets the data from the connectionStrings section of the configuration file.

SKILL SUMMARY

IN THIS LESSON YOU LEARNED:

- Delegates are special types that are used to encapsulate a method with a specific signature.
- Events are a way for an object to notify other objects or classes when something of interest happens. The object that sends the notification is called as a publisher of the event. The object that receives the notification is called the subscriber of the event.
- The .NET Framework supports standard exception handling to raise and handle runtime errors. To handle exceptions, place the code that throws exceptions inside a try block, and place the code that handles the different exceptions inside a list of catch blocks.

> * The `finally` block is used in association with the `try` block. The `finally` block is always executed regardless of whether an exception is thrown. The `finally` block is often used to write clean-up code.
> * Application settings allow the programs to change certain settings at runtime without the need to modify the program's source code.
> * The `WebConfigurationManager` class is the preferred way to work with configuration files related to Web applications. For client applications, use the `ConfigurationManager` class.

■ Knowledge Assessment

Fill in the Blank

Complete the following sentences by writing the correct word or words in the blanks provided.

1. The _____ block is often used in association with the `try` block to write cleanup code.

2. To handle exceptions, place the code that throws exceptions inside a _____ block and place the code that handles the exceptions inside _____ blocks.

3. When working with events, the class that sends the notification is called as a _____ of the event and the class that receives the notification is called the _____ of the event.

4. When passing event-related data from event publisher to event subscribers, use a class that is derived from the _____ class.

5. In the .NET Framework, an exception is represented by using an object of the _____ class or one of its derived classes.

6. When handling exceptions, the `catch` block should be written in order of the more _____ exception to the more _____ exceptions.

7. The applications settings are stored on the disk in _____ format.

8. A _____ is a type that references a method.

9. A delegate can be bound to any method whose signature matches that of the _____.

10. The _____ file allows the Web applications to change certain settings at runtime without the need to modify the application's source code.

Multiple Choice

Circle the letter that corresponds to the best answer.

1. You need to write code that closes a connection to a database. You need to make sure that this code is always executed regardless of whether an exception is thrown. Where should you write this code?
   a. Within a `try` block
   b. Within a `catch` block
   c. Within a `finally` block
   d. Within the `Main` method

2. You are writing code to handle events in your program. You defined a delegate named RectangleHandler like this:

```
public delegate void RectangleHandler(Rectangle rect);
```

You also create a variable of the RectangleHandler type like this:

```
RectangleHandler handler;
```

Later in the program, you need to add a method named DisplayArea to the method invocation list of the handler variable. The signature of the DisplayArea method matches with the signature of the RectangleHandler method. Any code that you write should not affect any existing event handling code. Which of the following code examples should you write?

a. `handler = new Rectanglehandler(DisplayArea);`
b. `handler = DisplayArea;`
c. `handler += DisplayArea;`
d. `handler -= DisplayArea;`

3. You are developing a Windows form that responds to mouse events. When the mouse moves, you need to invoke the method Form1_HandleMouse. Any code that you write should not affect any existing event handling code. Which of the following statements should you use to attach the event handler with the event?

a.
```
this.MouseDown = new MouseEventHandler
        (Form1_HandleMouse);
```
b.
```
this.MouseMove = new MouseEventHandler
        (Form1_HandleMouse);
```
c.
```
this.MouseDown += new MouseEventHandler
        (Form1_HandleMouse);
```
d.
```
this.MouseMove += new MouseEventHandler
        (Form1_HandleMouse);
```

4. What will be the output of the following code?

```
int num = 5;
int den = 0;
try
{
    Console.WriteLine("Performing Division");
    int res = num/den;
    Console.WriteLine("After Division");
}
catch(SystemException se)
{
    Console.WriteLine("In Catch Block");
}
Console.WriteLine("After Catch Block");
```
a.
```
Performing Division
After Catch Block
```

b.
```
Performing Division
After Division
In Catch Block
After Catch Block
```
c.
```
Performing Division
In Catch Block
After Catch Block
```
d.
```
Performing Division
In Catch Block
After Division
After Catch Block
```

5. You are developing a Windows Forms application using C#. Your application needs to query the name and address of the user. You have placed two TextBox controls named `txtName` and `txtAddress`. When the user presses a key on TextBox controls, or when the user changes the text in the TextBox controls, you want to run code to ensure that the user does not enters a numeric value.

    You are looking at responding to the `TextChanged` and `KeyPress` events. The event handler for `TextChanged` receives an argument of the `EventArgs` type while the `KeyPress` receives an argument of the `KeyPressEventArgs` type.

    You want to write minimum code. Which of the following best describes how to structure your code to fulfill this requirement?
    a. Write four separate event handlers, one each for the `TextChanged` event of `txtName`, the `KeyPress` event of `txtName`, the `TextChanged` event of `txtAddress`, and the `KeyPress` event of `txtAddress`.
    b. Write two event handlers. The first handles both `TextChanged` events, and the second handles both `KeyPress` events.
    c. Write two event handlers. The first handles the `TextChanged` and `KeyPress` events for `txtName`, and the second handles the `TextChanged` and `KeyPress` events for `txtAddress`.
    d. Write a single event handler to handle the `TextChanged` and `KeyPress` events of both controls.

6. You develop a Windows form application using C#. The name of the application's executable file is SalesAnalysis.exe. For easy configuration of the application, you decide to deploy the application with an application configuration file. At runtime, the Windows form application must be able to read the settings stored in the configuration file. Which of the following actions should you take? (Select all that apply)
    a. Name the configuration file as SalesAnalysis.config
    b. Name the configuration file as SalesAnalysis.exe.config
    c. Deploy the configuration file to the same directory as the executable file
    d. Deploy the configuration file to a child folder named config

7. You have developed an ASP.NET application. The application needs to retrieve orders from a warehouse. For the sake of flexibility, you store the warehouse name in the `<appSettings>` element in the web.config, application's configuration file. After you deploy the application to the production Web server, the administrator will be required to modify the configuration file to change the warehouse. You want the new settings to be applied as soon as possible. What action should the administrator take to ensure that the application reads the new connection string from the configuration file?

   a. Nothing. As soon as the administrator modifies and saves the configuration file, the application will automatically use the new warehouse name.

   b. Recompile the application

   c. Restart the ASP.NET process

   d. Close the application and restart the Web server

8. You are developing a Web application that processes orders. You need to store certain application parameters that can be configured without recompiling the application. Which of the following should you do? (Select all that apply)

   a. Store the configuration in app.config file.

   b. Store the configuration in web.config file.

   c. Use the `ConfigurationManager` class to access the settings from the configuration file.

   d. Use the `WebConfigurationManager` class to access the settings from the configuration file.

9. What will be the output of the following code?

```
int num = 5;
int den = 0;
try
{
    Console.WriteLine("First");
    int res = num/den;
    Console.WriteLine("Second");
}
catch(DivideByZeroException ex)
{
    Console.WriteLine("Third");
}
finally
{
    Console.WriteLine("Fourth");
}
    Console.WriteLine("Fifth");
```

   a.
```
First
Second
Third
Fourth
Fifth
```

   b.
```
First
Third
Fourth
Fifth
```

   c.
```
First
Second
Third
Fourth
```

   d.
```
First
Third
Fifth
```

10. You are developing a console application that reads data from the file. Your application needs to handle all exceptions, including when the file is not found. You write the following code (line numbers are for reference only):

```
01: StreamReader sr = null;
02: try
03: {
04:     sr = File.OpenText(@"c:\data.txt");
05:     Console.WriteLine(sr.ReadToEnd());
06: }
07: catch (FileNotFoundException fnfe)
08: {
09:     Console.WriteLine(fnfe.Message);
10: }
11: catch (Exception ex)
12: {
13:     Console.WriteLine(ex.Message);
14: }
```

You need to write code to close the StreamReader object. You need to make sure that StreamReader object is always closed, whether an exception was thrown or not. What should you do?

a. Insert the following code after line 05:

```
sr.Close();
```

b. Insert the following code after line 09:

```
sr.Close();
```

c. Insert the following code after line 13:

```
sr.Close();
```

d. Insert the following code after line 14:

```
finally
{
    sr.Close();
}
```

■ Competency Assessment

Project 3-1: Accessing Application Settings for Windows Forms Application

You are developing a Windows Forms application. You should provide an application-level setting that allows the users to configure the background color of the application. The changes should not require modification to the source code. How should you achieve this?

Project 3-2: Handling the MouseDown Event

You are developing a game that allows users to hit target areas on a Windows Form with mouse. You need to develop an experimental form that displays the X and Y coordinates of the location clicked by the user in the form's title bar. How should you achieve this?

■ **Proficiency Assessment**

Project 3-3: Handle Exceptions

You are writing code for a simple arithmetic library. You decide to create a method named `Divide` that takes two arguments (x and y), and returns the value of x/y. You need to catch any arithmetic exceptions that might be thrown for errors in arithmetic, casting, or data type conversions. You also need to catch any other exceptions that might be thrown from the code. How should you create proper structured exception handling code to address this requirement?

Project 3-4: Creating and Handling Events

You are writing code for creating and handling events in your program. The `SampleClass` class needs to implement the following interface:

```
public delegate void SampleDelegate();
public interface ISampleEvents
{
    event SampleDelegate SampleEvent;
    void Invoke();
}
```

How should you write code for the `SampleClass` and for a test method that creates an instance of the `SampleClass` and invokes the event?

4 LESSON

Understanding Code Compilation and Deployment

EXAM OBJECTIVE MATRIX

SKILLS/CONCEPTS	MTA EXAM OBJECTIVE	MTA EXAM OBJECTIVE NUMBER
Understanding Code Compilation	Understand the fundamentals of Microsoft Intermediate Language (MSIL) and Common Language Infrastructure (CLI).	3.1
Understanding Assemblies and Metadata	Understand the use of strong naming.	3.2
	Understand assemblies and metadata.	3.4
Understanding Code Deployment	Understand version control.	3.3

KEY TERMS

assembly

assembly manifest

Common Intermediate Language (CIL)

Common Language Infrastructure (CLI)

Common Language Runtime (CLR)

Common Language Specification (CLS)

Common Type System (CTS)

compilation

delay signing

Global Assembly Cache (GAC)

Just-in-Time (JIT) compilation

language interoperability

metadata

Microsoft Intermediate Language (MSIL)

private assembly

private key

public key

publisher policy

shared assembly

side-by-side execution

strong name

Virtual Execution System (VES)

You are a software developer for the Northwind Corporation. As part of your job, you develop computer programs to solve business problems. In order to be effective at your work, you need to understand how the code is compiled and deployed.

You need to understand how to create a strong name for an assembly and how to deploy assemblies to the global assembly cache. You'll also need to know how to version your components and configure your applications in such a way that you can target the use of a specific version of an assembly.

Understanding Code Compilation

↓
THE BOTTOM LINE

Computer programs are generally written in a high-level language such as C# and Visual Basic. However, the computer can only understand machine language. A code written in high-level programming language must be translated to the machine language before it can be executed. This translation is also known as *compilation*. This section explores how the code compilation works in the .NET Framework.

CERTIFICATION READY
What is the Common Language Infrastructure (CLI)?
3.1

Traditionally, for high-level programming languages such as C or C++, the compilation model looks similar to Figure 4-1.

Figure 4-1

The traditional compilation model

Here, the language compiler processes the source code and translates it into machine code. Once translated, the code can directly be executed by the computer. However, for the languages targeting the .NET Framework, compilation is a two-step process (see Figure 4-2).

Figure 4-2

Code compilation in the .NET Framework

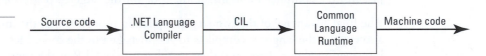

In the case of .NET Framework, a program in a higher-level programming language such as C# or Visual Basic is first compiled to the *Common Intermediate Language (CIL)*. CIL is an intermediate language that sits between the high-level programming language and the machine code. CIL can't be directly understood by the processor, but it can be efficiently converted to processor-specific code. You might think of .NET language compilers as half-compilers because rather than converting the programs completely to the machine code, they convert the programs to an intermediate language. The output from language compiler is usually in form of a .dll or .exe file. On the .NET Framework, these files contain the CIL code rather than the processor-specific code.

TAKE NOTE *

Common Intermediate Language (CIL) was formerly known as *Microsoft Intermediate Language (MSIL)*. MSIL was renamed CIL after it was accepted as an international standard by Ecma International (an international standards organization). At the time of this writing, the exam objective for this exam still refers CIL as MSIL. When you see the term MSIL, it actually refers to CIL.

The second half of the compilation process doesn't happen until the program is ready for execution. The **Common Language Runtime** (CLR) is a part of the .NET Framework that is responsible for manging the execution of the programs. The CLR uses a process called **Just-in-Time (JIT) compilation** to convert the CIL code into the code specifically targeted to a particular processor architecture. In the .NET Framework, this processor-specific code is often referred to as the native code. The JIT compilation process is independent of the original programming language because the original program has already been translated into CIL.

The first advantages of the two-step compilation process is that rather than writing a full compiler for each programming language, the language designers need only write a "half-compiler" to convert the code from a high-level programming language to CIL (see Figure 4-3). The second half of the compiler that translates CIL to native code is already a part of the .NET Framework.

Figure 4-3

Compiling multiple languages in the .NET Framework

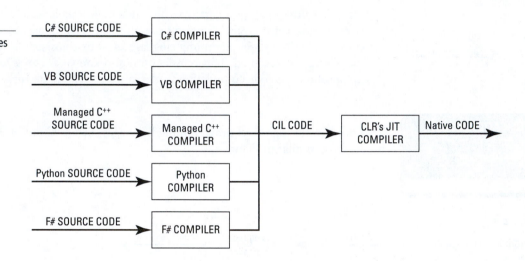

The second advantage of the two-step compilation process is that after you have compiled the code to the common intermediate language, you don't have to do anything to target different processor architecture as long as the common language runtime supports that processor architecture. Once you copy the CIL code to the desired .NET Framework version, the just-in-time compiler will translate the code for the targeted processor architecture.

The final advantage of the two-step compilation process is that the intermediate translation also enables the language compilers to add metadata to the code. Metadata provides additional information about classes and their members to the CLR at the runtime.

Understanding Common Language Infrastructure (CLI)

The **Common Language Infrastructure (CLI)** is an international standard approved by ISO and Ecma International. The CLI standard provides the specifications for the executable code and the runtime environment in which the code runs.

The objective of the CLI is to make it easier to write components and applications in any language. It does this by defining a standard set of types by making all components fully self-describing and by providing an execution environment. All CLI-compliant components are accessible to all CLI-aware languages and tools.

The CLI standard provides specifications for the following:

- **Common Type System (CTS):** CTS defines the rules for declaring, using, and managing data types and their operations. CTS helps with language integration and allows for objects written in one language to be used by objects written in another language as if they were written in the same language.

- *Common Language Specification (CLS):* CLS defines the rules for programming language features. These are the rules that a language must comply with in order to interoperate with other CLS-compliant programming languages.

- **Metadata:** The metadata is a structured way to represent information about a program structure that the CLI uses to locate and load classes at runtime.

- *Virtual Execution System (VES):* VES specifies how the runtime loads and executes CLI-compatible programs. VES provides the services needed to execute code, using the metadata to connect separately generated code at runtime. When the code is executed, the platform-specific VES compiles the CIL to the machine language according to the specific hardware and operating system.

The *Common Language Runtime (CLR)* is Microsoft's implementation of the CLI. As CLI now is a well-defined standard, it opens a path for additional implementation of CLI outside of Microsoft. The Mono project led by Xamarin is one such implementation. Mono is cross-platform and can be run on a variety of operating systems (such as Linux, Android, and iOS).

Understanding Language Interoperability

> *Language interoperability* is a feature of .NET Framework that enables the code written in a programming language to interact with code written in a different programming language.

The .NET Framework provides support for language interoperability. Language interoperability means that code written in one programming language can be fully used by code written in a different programming language. As a result, .NET Framework developers can possibly write portions of their applications by using different programming languages. Developers can do their usual programming tasks (such as inheriting from a type, instantiating a type, or calling methods on a type) without concerning themselves with what language a type was written with.

Even tools such as debuggers and profilers do provide support for language interoperability. For example, when debugging a C# programmer, the Visual Studio debugger can step right into the code for a component that was written into Visual Basic.

When used effectively, language interoperability can help improve the development process. Developers can use the language of their choice and once the code is written, that language can be used across many applications without porting it over to a different language.

CLS specifies a set of rules that enables the code written in a programming language to inter-operate with the code written in other programming languages on the .NET Framework. If language interoperability is your requirement, you should use only CLS-compliant features of a programming language.

TAKE NOTE*

Language interoperability is a run-time feature. You can't mix and match different programming languages as a single compilation unit. A compiler can only compile code written in one programming language. However, you can certainly have an assembly in which all code was written in C# interoperate with another assembly in which all code was written using Visual Basic. For the same reason, when you create a Visual Studio Project, you can use only one programming language in the project. It has to be compiled by a single language compiler. You can, of course, add references to other projects in which code was written in a different programming language.

■ Understanding Assemblies and Metadata

↓
THE BOTTOM LINE An *assembly* is a library of compiled code and is the fundamental unit of deployment, version control, and security configuration in the .NET Framework. Depending on how assemblies are deployed, there are two types of assemblies: private and shared.

CERTIFICATION READY
What is an assembly?
3.4

An assembly is a collection of types and resources that is built to work together to form a logical unit of functionality. Assemblies are the fundamental unit of deployment, version control, and security in the .NET Framework.

When you compile a program by using a .NET language compiler, the output in the form of a .dll file or an .exe file is bundled into an assembly. An assembly can be contained within a single physical file or it can span multiple physical files. Generally speaking, an assembly contains the following four pieces of information:

- *Assembly manifest*, which contains information such as version and identity of the assembly
- Metadata related to the classes contained in the assembly
- CIL code that implements the classes
- A set of resources (such as .bmp file or a .jpg file) used by the classes

Understanding Metadata

Metadata is the data that describes the types defined by the code and the external types used by the code. Metadata has complete information about the structure of a type and its members. For example, metadata includes the method parameters and return types of a method.

The compiler produces metadata when the code is compiled. Metadata is independent of any particular programming language and is stored along with the CIL as part of an assembly.

Execution of code by the VES is metadata-driven. The VES uses the metadata to provide services such as creating instances of the types and memory management. Metadata also provides a common interchange mechanism for use between tools that manipulate programs (such as compilers and debuggers) as well as between these tools and the VES.

The information available as part of metadata is valuable for getting information about the code after the code is compiled. The .NET Framework provides a set of classes as part of the `System.Reflection` namespace that provides a logical view of the metadata. You can use the reflection API to inspect code and dynamically invoke methods at runtime.

The metadata in the assembly and the reflection library is also used by various code analysis tools to inspect and decompile the code. You will learn about two of these tools in this section:

- The Intermediate Language Disassembler (ildasm.exe) is part of the .NET Framework software development kit (SDK). This tool allows you to view the contents of an assembly like the manifest, metadata and the CIL.
- ILSpy (available from http://wiki.sharpdevelop.net/ILSpy.ashx) is a non-Microsoft tool that not only helps you browse the contents of an assembly, it can decompile the CIL back to the source code.

➡ **LOOK INSIDE ASSEMBLIES**

GET READY. To take a look inside assemblies by using ildasm.exe and ilspy.exe, perform the following steps:

1. Create a new Console Application project and name the project as CurrentTime.

2. Replace the code for the default `Program` class with the following:

```
class Program
{
    static void Main(string[] args)
    {
        Console.WriteLine(
            "The current time is: {0}",
            DateTime.Now);
    }
}
```

3. Build the project.

4. Run the ildasm.exe program. You can find this program in the Visual Studio SDK Tools folder or you can use the Windows search feature to look for ildasm.exe.

5. In the ildasm.exe's user interface, click **File > Open** and then browse to the CurrentTime.exe file (this file is in the project's output folder). Once the file loaded, you will see an interface similar to Figure 4-4.

Figure 4-4

The Intermediate Language Disassembler tool

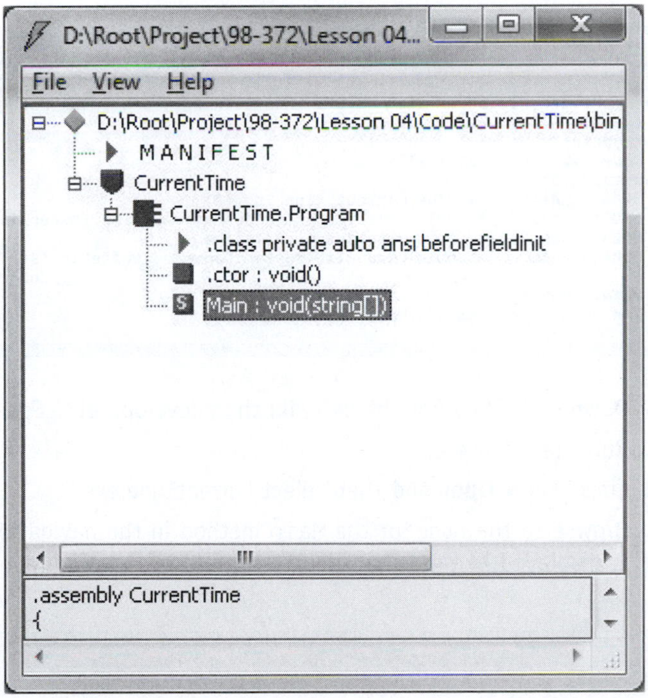

```
D:\Root\Project\98-372\Lesson 04...

File   View   Help

⊟─◆ D:\Root\Project\98-372\Lesson 04\Code\CurrentTime\bin
    ▶ M A N I F E S T
  ⊟─🛡 CurrentTime
    ⊟─▣ CurrentTime.Program
        ▶ .class private auto ansi beforefieldinit
        ■ .ctor : void()
        S Main : void(string[])




◀        |||                ▶
.assembly CurrentTime
{
◀                          ▶
```

6. Notice that the program displays the logical structure of the assembly in a hierarchical view. Double-click the MANIFEST node and the Assembly Manifest displays (see Figure 4-5).

Figure 4-5

Viewing the Assembly Manifest by using ildasm.exe

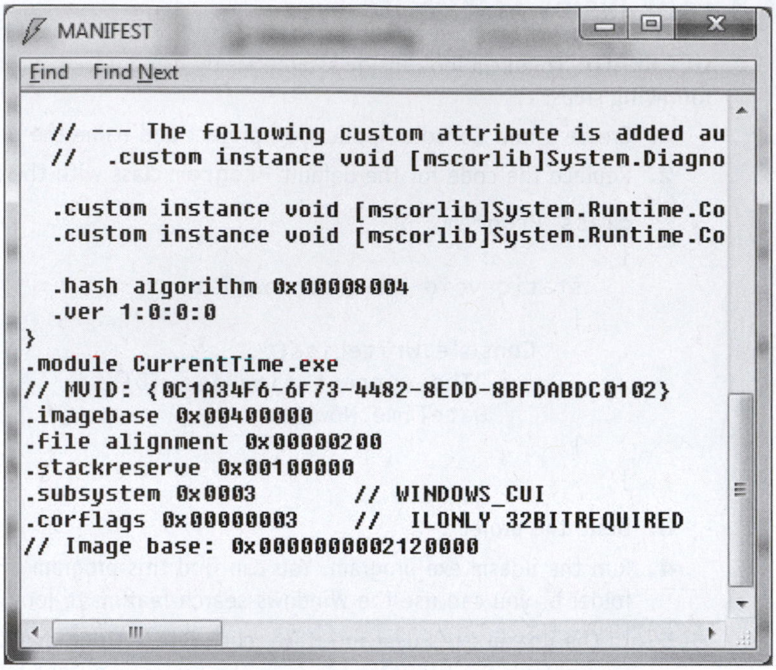
MANIFEST
Find Find Next
// --- The following custom attribute is added au
// .custom instance void [mscorlib]System.Diagno
.custom instance void [mscorlib]System.Runtime.Co
.custom instance void [mscorlib]System.Runtime.Co
.hash algorithm 0x00008004
.ver 1:0:0:0
}
.module CurrentTime.exe
// MVID: {0C1A34F6-6F73-4482-8EDD-8BFDABDC0102}
.imagebase 0x00400000
.file alignment 0x00000200
.stackreserve 0x00100000
.subsystem 0x0003 // WINDOWS_CUI
.corflags 0x00000003 // ILONLY 32BITREQUIRED
// Image base: 0x0000000002120000

7. In ildasm.exe's interface, double-click the node for the `Main` method. The CIL corresponding to the code in the `Main` method is displayed as shown in Figure 4-6.

Figure 4-6

Viewing the CIL by using the ildasm.exe

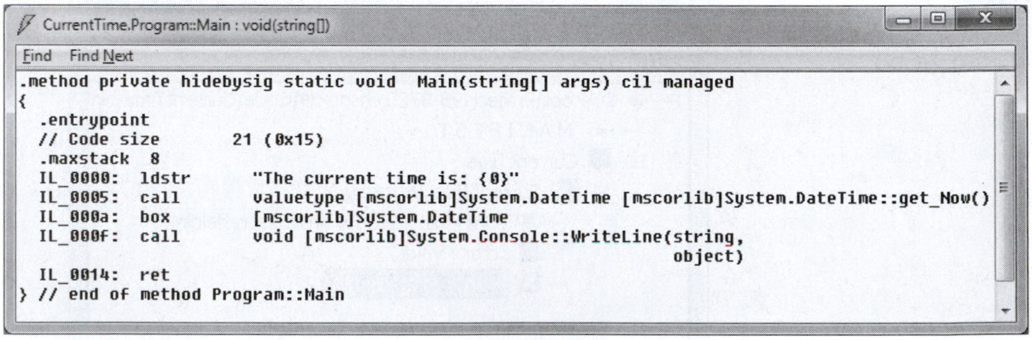
CurrentTime.Program::Main : void(string[])
Find Find Next
.method private hidebysig static void Main(string[] args) cil managed
{
.entrypoint
// Code size 21 (0x15)
.maxstack 8
IL_0000: ldstr "The current time is: {0}"
IL_0005: call valuetype [mscorlib]System.DateTime [mscorlib]System.DateTime::get_Now()
IL_000a: box [mscorlib]System.DateTime
IL_000f: call void [mscorlib]System.Console::WriteLine(string, object)
IL_0014: ret
} // end of method Program::Main

8. Download ILSpy from http://wiki.sharpdevelop.net/ILSpy.ashx.
9. Run the ILSpy.exe.
10. Click **File > Open** and then select CurrentTime.exe.
11. Browse to the node for the `Main` method in the navigation tree. The decompiled code is displayed in the right side of the window (see Figure 4-7).

Figure 4-7

Decompiling the source code by using the ILSpy.exe

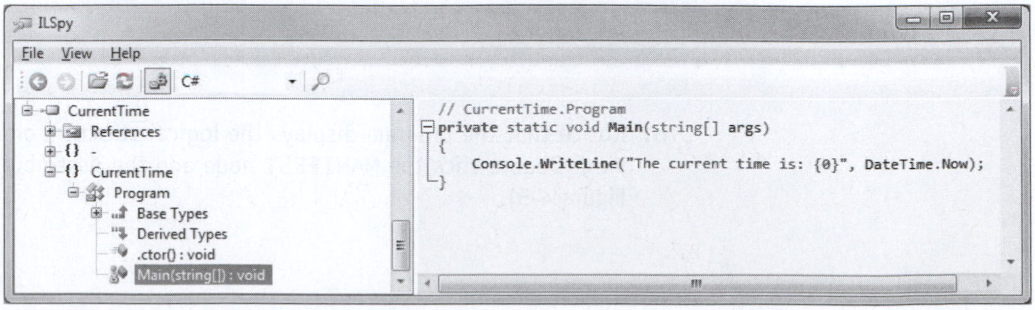
ILSpy
File View Help
C#
CurrentTime
References
{} -
{} CurrentTime
Program
Base Types
Derived Types
.ctor() : void
Main(string[]) : void
// CurrentTime.Program
private static void Main(string[] args)
{
Console.WriteLine("The current time is: {0}", DateTime.Now);
}

Understanding Private Assemblies

A *private assembly* is local to the application that uses it and is deployed within the application's directory structure. Private assemblies are designed to be used by only a single application. Any changes to a private assembly cannot possibly affect any other installed application on the same machine. The .NET Framework does not impose any special versioning or naming requirements for a private assembly.

TAKE NOTE[*]

The .NET Framework does not require assemblies to be registered in the Windows Registry. Applications that use private assemblies can be simply deployed by using the XCOPY command.

Consider an application, BusinessApp.exe, that uses a private assembly, UIComponents.dll. In version 1 of the application, you can deploy both the files to a directory such as C:\Program Files\BusinessApp\v1.0. When you release a second version of the application, you can choose to deploy all of its files into a different directory structure, such as C:\Program Files\ BusinessApp\v2.0. In this case, each version is independent of each other and also independent of any other application on the same machine.

You can specify a version for an assembly by using the assembly-level `AssemblyVersion` attribute. However, for a private assembly, this version information is for informational purposes only; the common language runtime does not use it to bind to a specific version of the assembly. As shown in the previous example, versioning of a private assembly can be as simple as deploying each version to a different location.

By default, all assemblies in the .NET Framework are created as private assemblies.

Understanding Shared Assemblies

An assembly that can be referenced by more than one application is called as a *shared assembly*. The shared assemblies are all installed at a common, well-known location on the file system known as the Global Assembly Cache (GAC), which is covered later in this lesson. To avoid deployment problems, the .NET Framework allows multiple versions of a shared assembly to coexist. The .NET Framework also protects assemblies from different publishers from overwriting each other.An assembly must meet the following requirements to be deployed as a shared assembly:

- A shared assembly must have an associated strong name.
- A shared assembly must be installed in GAC.

Understanding Strong Naming

CERTIFICATION READY
What is the role of a strong name?
3.2

Strong name specifies an assembly's unique identity. Strong name is used to make sure that the applications can precisely refer to an assembly, thereby avoiding any conflicts in name, version, or publisher.

If shared assemblies are identified by just their names—as the private assemblies are—two software publishers theoretically could use the same name for an assembly. Even the same software publisher can have multiple versions of an assembly. These situations can lead to problems in deployment and execution. For example, if a newer version of an assembly overwrites an older version, any application that depends on the older version will fail. Similarly, you do not want your application to accidentally refer to code from different publisher just because it shares the same name.

To ensure applications are deployed and executed correctly, there has to be a more precise way to identify an assembly. The .NET Framework provides a solution to this problem in the form of strong names. The .NET Framework requires all shared assemblies to have a strong name.

A strong name uses four attributes to identify an assembly:

- Simple name
- Version number
- Culture identity (optional)
- Public key token

To create a strong name, you need an assembly's simple name, its version number, an optional culture identity, and a key pair.

The key pair consists of two related pieces of binary data: a public key and a private key. The *public key* is the key that represents the identity of a software publisher and can be shared. When you create a strongly named assembly, the public key is stored in the assembly manifest, along with other identification information (such as name, version number, and culture). This scheme does not look foolproof because the public key is easily available from the assembly manifest, and an assembly identity easily can be faked with some other company's public key. To verify that only the legitimate owner of the public key has created the assembly, an assembly is signed with the publisher's private key. The *private key* is the key used for signatures and is assumed to be known only to the assembly's publisher.

The process of signing an assembly and verifying its signature works like this:

- **Signing an assembly:** When you sign an assembly, a cryptographic hash of the assembly's contents is computed. The hash is then encoded with the private key and is stored within the assembly. The public key is stored in the assembly manifest.
- **Verifying the signature:** When the common language runtime verifies an assembly's identity, it reads the public key from the assembly manifest and uses it to decrypt the cryptographic hash that is stored in the assembly. It then recalculates the hash for the current contents of the assembly. If the two hashes match, this ensures two things: The contents of the assembly were not tampered with after the assembly was signed, and only the party that has a private key associated with the public key stored in the assembly has signed the assembly.

TAKE NOTE*

To learn more about public and private key cryptography, please refer to Lesson 6.

You can generate public/private key pairs by using the command-line Strong Name tool (sn.exe). The following exercise shows you how to use the strong name tool to generate a key pair.

⊕ USE THE STRONG NAME TOOL

GET READY. To use the strong name tool to generate a key pair, perform the following steps:

1. Click **Start > Microsoft Visual Studio 2010 > Visual Studio Tools > Visual Studio Command Prompt.**
2. Type the following command and then press **Enter:**

   ```
   sn.exe –k test.snk
   ```

   This command generates a new key pair and then writes it to a file named test.snk (see Figure 4-8).

Figure 4-8

Using the Strong Name tool to generate a key file

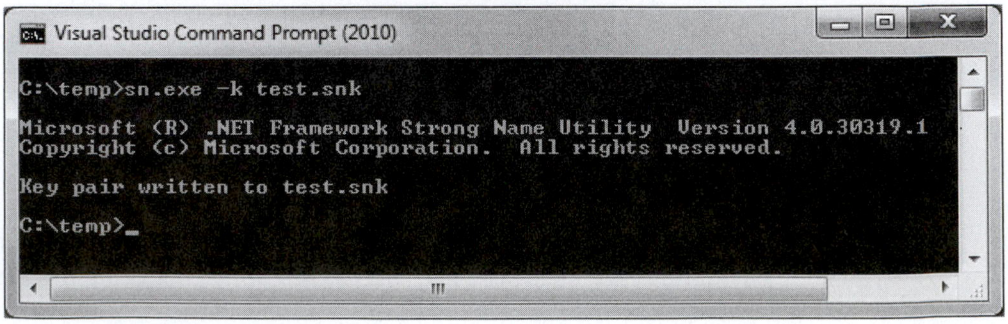

```
Visual Studio Command Prompt (2010)

C:\temp>sn.exe -k test.snk

Microsoft (R) .NET Framework Strong Name Utility   Version 4.0.30319.1
Copyright (c) Microsoft Corporation.   All rights reserved.

Key pair written to test.snk

C:\temp>_
```

3. Browse to the folder to verify that the test.snk file is created. This file contains both the private key and the public key.

Once you generate a key file, you can use the file to create an assembly with a strong name. The following exercise shows how to create an assembly with a strong name.

➜ ASSIGN A STRONG NAME TO AN ASSEMBLY

GET READY. To create an assembly with a strong name, perform the following steps:

1. Create a new Visual Studio project based on the Class Library template and name the project as MathUtil.

2. Rename the default code file Class1.cs to RandomNumber.cs.

3. Replace the code in RandomNumber.cs with the following:

```
using System;

namespace MathUtil
{
    public class RandomNumber
    {
        public int MinValue { get; set; }
        public int MaxValue { get; set; }

        public RandomNumber()
        {
            MinValue = int.MinValue;
            MaxValue = int.MaxValue;
        }

        public int Get()
        {
            Random r = new Random();
            return r.Next(MinValue, MaxValue);
        }
    }
}
```

4. Click **Project > Add Existing Item.**

5. In the Add Existing Item dialog box, make sure that the file filter is set to All Files (*.*) so that you can see all files. Browse to the test.snk file created in the previous exercise and then click the Add button to add the file to the project.

6. Click **Project > MathUtil Properties.**

7. Click **Signing,** check the **Sign the assembly** option, and then choose the test.snk file from the drop-down list (see Figure 4-9).

Figure 4-9

Signing an assembly with the strong name

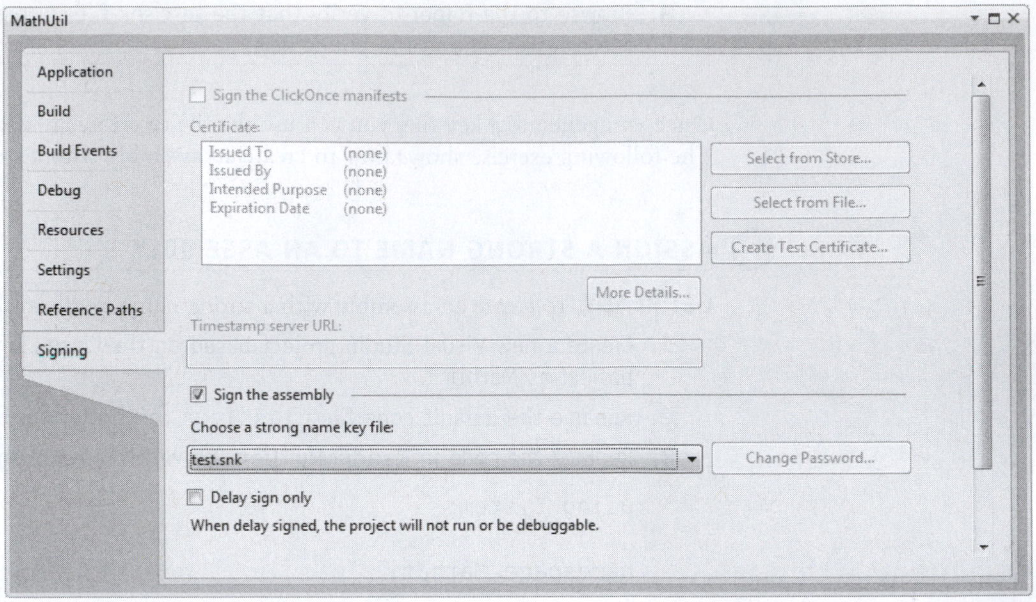

8. In the same MathUtil Properties dialog box, select **Application** and then click the **Assembly Information** button. You will see a dialog box as shown in Figure 4-10. Notice that you can use this dialog box to change the assembly information such as the **Assembly version**, the culture (via the **Neutral language** setting), the **Copyright** information, and so on. The **GUID** is a globally unique identifier for the assembly and it will be different for your project.

Figure 4-10

Using the Assembly Information dialog box

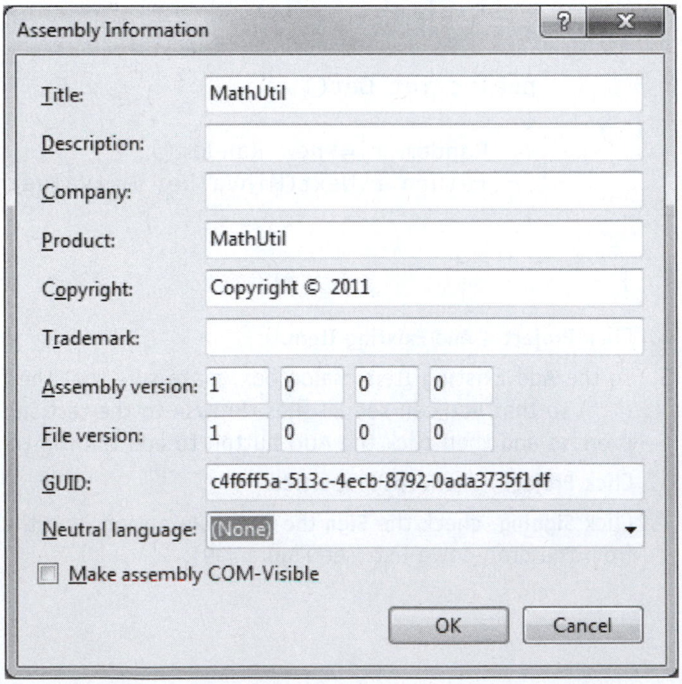

9. Close the dialog box.

10. Build the project. The project's output MathUtil.dll is now a strongly named assembly.

Using Delay Signing

The key pair that is generated with sn.exe contained both the public key and private key. For most organizations, the private key is usually a closely-guarded secret with only a few people having access to it. These organizations follow a practice called delay signing. In *delay signing*, only the public key is extracted from the key pair and stored in a separate file. Then only the public key is used for development and testing. When the code is ready for packaging, the assemblies are signed with private key.

In the previous exercise, you created test.snk, which contained both the public and the private key for the organization. The following command uses the option "-p" to extract the public key from the test.snk file and store it in the publickey.snk file:

```
sn.exe -p test.snk publickey.snk
```

Now you can start using publickey.snk rather than test.snk to sign your code for development and testing.

However, any assembly that you sign with only the public key is a potential for security vulnerability and therefore will not pass the .NET Framework security verification. For development and testing purpose, you can register an assembly for skipping the security verification by using the -Vr option of sn.exe as follows:

```
sn.exe -Vr MathUtil.dll
```

When the development and testing is over, you can unregister the for verification skipping by using the -Vu option as follows:

```
sn.exe -Vu MathUtil.dll
```

Finally, when you are ready for shipping, you can sign an assembly again with the key pair file by using the -R option of sn.exe as follows:

```
sn.exe -R MathUtil.dll test.snk
```

■ Understanding Code Deployment

THE BOTTOM LINE

Software deployment is a set of activities performed in order to make the software ready for use. These activities may involve copying the files to their correct locations and making sure that the correct version of the software is being used.

Assemblies can be deployed either as private assemblies or shared assemblies. Shared assemblies must be deployed to the global assembly cache. In this section, you'll learn how to install assemblies to the Global Assembly Cache (GAC) and how to support side-by-side installation of different versions of an assembly.

Using the Global Assembly Cache (GAC)

The *Global Assembly Cache (GAC)* is the central repository for storing shared assemblies on a computer. The GAC simplifies deployment by allowing multiple versions of an assembly to co-exist.

A regular Windows folder can only differentiate files based on their simple names, not their strong names. Therefore, you need a special type of storage to store strongly-named assemblies in a well-known shared location. The .NET Framework provides this storage in the form of the GAC. For the .NET Framework 4.0, the GAC is located in the %windir%\Microsoft.NET\assembly\folder. Here %windir% is the location of the Windows installation directory. In addition to providing a shared location, the GAC provides the following benefits for shared assemblies:

- **Integrity check:** When assemblies are installed in the GAC, the GAC applies a strong integrity check on the assembly. This check guarantees that the contents of the assembly have not been changed since it was built.
- **Security:** The GAC enables only users with administrator privileges to modify its contents.
- **Side-by-side versioning:** Multiple assemblies with the same name but different version numbers can be maintained in the GAC.

After you have associated a strong name with an assembly, you can place the assembly in the GAC. There are two ways you can add an assembly to the GAC:

- By using the Windows Installer. This is the recommended approach for installing assemblies on the end user's computer.
- By using the Global Assembly Cache tool (gacutil.exe), a developer tool that is provided as part of the Windows Software Development Kit (SDK). You should use this tool only for development and testing purpose.

The following exercise shows you how to work with the GAC tool.

⊕ USE THE GLOBAL ASSEMBLY CACHE TOOL

GET READY. To learn how to use the GAC tool, perform the following steps:

1. Click **Start > Microsoft Visual Studio 2010 > Visual Studio Tools.** Right-click **Visual Studio Command Prompt** and then choose **Run as Administrator** from the shortcut menu.

2. Change the path to the location of the MathUtil.dll file that was created in the previous exercise.

3. Run the `gacutil.exe` command with the /i option, as follows, to add the MathUtil.dll file to the global assembly cache:

   `gacutil /i MathUtil.dll`

4. Notice the message indicating that the assembly is successfully added to the cache.

5. You can verify that the assembly is added to the GAC by using the /l option of gacutil.exe as follows.

   `gacutil /l MathUtil`

   The output of the gacutil program with option /l is shown in Figure 4-11.

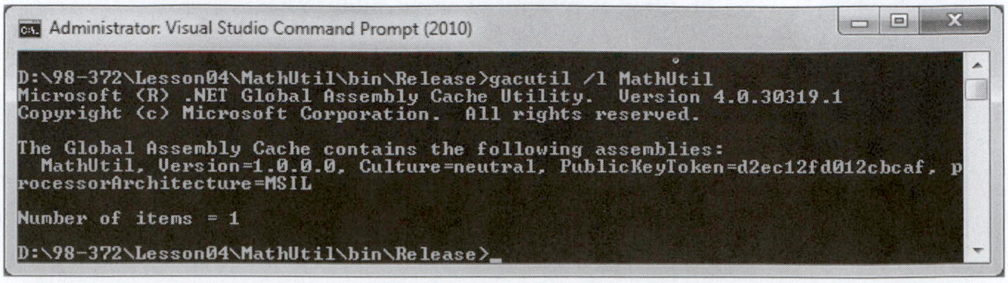

Figure 4-11

Verifying that an assembly exists in the GAC by using the gacutil.exe tool

6. Notice that gacutil.exe lists the assembly with all of its identifying details, such as name, version, culture, and public key token. The culture specifies information, such as the language, country/region, associated with the assembly. The `PublicKeyToken` information comes from the strong name file and will be different for each publisher. If there is more than one assembly in the GAC with the same name, they will be all listed as a result of this command.

You can remove an assembly from the GAC by using the `gacutil.exe` command with the `/u` option as follows:

```
gacutil /u MathUtil
```

Here again, you need only to provide the name of the assembly and not the file. Also, if there are multiple assemblies in the GAC with the same name, you'll need to provide additional details (such as version, culture, and public key token) to uninstall the assembly from the GAC:

```
gacutil /u MathUtil, Version=1.0.0.0, Culture=neutral,
PublicKeyToken=d2ec12fd012cbcaf, processorArchitecture=MSIL
```

Normally, when you refer to an assembly in a Visual Studio Project, you invoke the Add Reference dialog box and browse to the desired assembly. But you cannot simply browse to the assembly in the GAC. So, at compile time, you still need to access the copy of the assembly file that you have in a regular folder.

In the following exercise, you learn how to write an application that calls the `MathUtil` assembly from the GAC at runtime.

➔ INVOKE AN ASSEMBLY FROM GAC AT RUNTIME

GET READY. To invoke the `MathUtil` assembly from the GAC, perform the following steps:

1. Add a new Console Application project named Application1.
2. Click **Project > Add Reference**.
3. In the Add Reference dialog box, select the **Projects** tab and then select the **MathUtil** project.
4. Replace the code in the Program.cs file with the following code:

```csharp
using System;
using MathUtil;

namespace Application1
{
    class Program
    {
        static void Main(string[] args)
        {
            RandomNumber r = new RandomNumber
            {
                MinValue = 0,
                MaxValue = 500
            };
            Console.WriteLine(r.Get());
        }
    }
}
```

5. Set `Application1` as the startup project. Build and run the program.

6. The program will call the `MathUtil` assembly from GAC at runtime and display the generated random number.

Understanding Version Control

> Multiple versions of a shared assembly can co-exist in the GAC. When you have multiple versions of an assembly installed in the GAC, you can configure an application to use a specific version of the assembly. In this section, you'll learn how to configure applications to control what version of the assemblies are used.

CERTIFICATION READY
What is side-by-side execution?
3.3

When you are creating shared components that are used by multiple applications, there are two common scenarios that will lead you to create a new version for an assembly:

- You have added additional features in the new version—some applications might still want to use the old version of the assembly but other applications might want to benefit from the new functionality provided in the new version. This execution model is also referred to as *side-by-side execution*.

- You found some critical defects in the assembly that you shipped—you fix the defects and release a new version. You want all the applications that reference the defective version of the assembly to start using the new version—and preferably without any modifications to the installed applications. This can be achieved by setting a publisher policy for the assembly.

The .NET Framework application configuration and assembly binding features allow you to handle both of these scenarios.

Understanding Side-by-Side Execution

> Consider a scenario in which you have an application named Application1 that uses version 1.0 of the `MathUtil` shared assembly. When a new version 1.1 of `MathUtil` is released, you install it to the GAC as well.

The following exercise shows you how to add multiple versions of an assembly to the GAC.

⊙ ADD MULTIPLE VERSIONS OF AN ASSEMBLY TO THE GAC

GET READY. To add multiple versions of an assembly to the GAC, perform the following steps:

1. Open the MathUtil project that you created earlier in this lesson.

2. Replace the code in the RandomNumber.cs file with the following code:

```
using System;
using System.Diagnostics;

namespace MathUtils
{
    public class RandomNumber
    {
        public int MinValue { get; set; }
        public int MaxValue { get; set; }
```

```
        public RandomNumber()
        {
            MinValue = int.MinValue;
            MaxValue = int.MaxValue;
        }

        // Get the next random number and
        // create an entry in the event log
        public int Get()
        {
            Random r = new Random();
            int random = r.Next(MinValue, MaxValue);

            EventLog eventLog = new EventLog();
            eventLog.Source =
                "MathUtil.RandomNumber v1.1";
            eventLog.WriteEntry(
                "Random Number: " + random);
            return random;
        }
    }
}
```

3. Click **Project > MathUtil Properties**. On the **Application** tab, click the **Assembly Information** button.

4. In the Assembly Information dialog box, change the minor version of the assembly, making the **Assembly version** 1.1.0.0 (see Figure 4-12). A unique GUID identifies the assembly. Neutral language specifies which culture the assembly supports. The default is none meaning that the assembly is not tied to a particular geographic region.

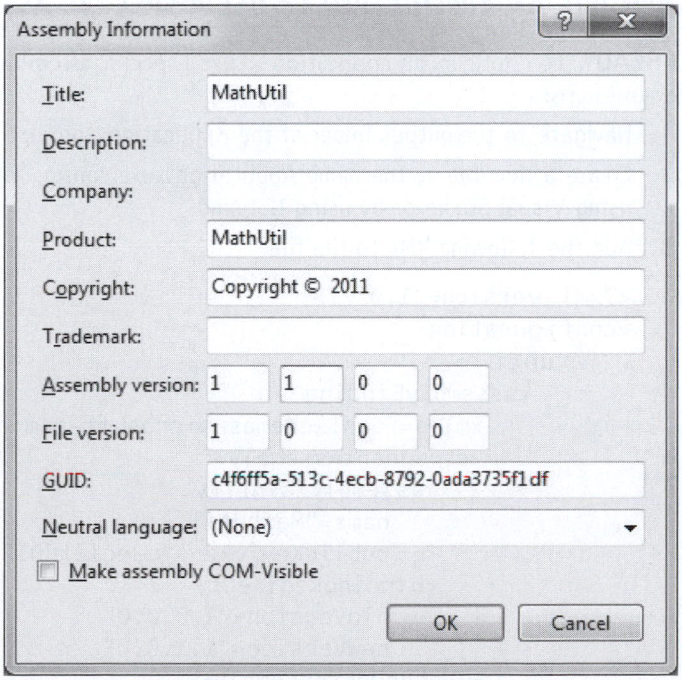

Figure 4-12

Changing the Assembly version for the MathUtil assembly

Assembly Information				
Title:	MathUtil			
Description:				
Company:				
Product:	MathUtil			
Copyright:	Copyright © 2011			
Trademark:				
Assembly version:	1	1	0	0
File version:	1	0	0	0
GUID:	c4f6ff5a-513c-4ecb-8792-0ada3735f1df			
Neutral language:	(None)			

☐ Make assembly COM-Visible

OK   Cancel

5. Build the MathUtil project.

6. Open the Visual Studio command prompt in administrative mode and change the path to the MathUtil project's output folder.

7. Run the `gacutil.exe` command with the `/i` option, as follows, to add the new version of the `MathUtil` assembly to the global assembly cache:

```
gacutil /i MathUtil.dll
```

8. Run the `gacutil` command with the `/l` option to verify that both the versions of the `MathUtil` assembly exist in the global assembly cache:

```
gacutil /l MathUtil
```

As shown in Figure 4-13, you will see both the versions of the assembly.

Figure 4-13

Listing all versions of the MathUtil Assembly in the GAC

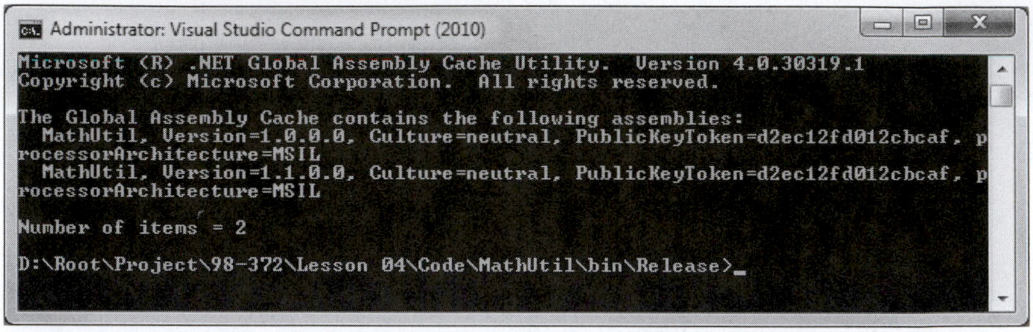

```
Administrator: Visual Studio Command Prompt (2010)

Microsoft (R) .NET Global Assembly Cache Utility.  Version 4.0.30319.1
Copyright (c) Microsoft Corporation.  All rights reserved.

The Global Assembly Cache contains the following assemblies:
  MathUtil, Version=1.0.0.0, Culture=neutral, PublicKeyToken=d2ec12fd012cbcaf, p
rocessorArchitecture=MSIL
  MathUtil, Version=1.1.0.0, Culture=neutral, PublicKeyToken=d2ec12fd012cbcaf, p
rocessorArchitecture=MSIL

Number of items = 2

D:\Root\Project\98-372\Lesson 04\Code\MathUtil\bin\Release>
```

At this point, the Application1 project is still using version 1.0 of the `MathUtil` assembly because that's what it was compiled with. How do you configure Application1 in such a way that it starts using the new version 1.1 of the `MathUtil` assembly, without recompiling the application and without affecting any other applications that might be still accessing the old version of the assembly? One way is to modify the application configuration file for just Application1. Changes to the application configuration affect only a particular application and do not need recompilation. The following exercise shows you how to do this.

CONFIGURE AN APPLICATION TO USE A SPECIFIC ASSEMBLY VERSION

GET READY. To configure an application to use a specific assembly version, perform the following steps:

1. Navigate to the output folder of the Application1 project.
2. Create a new file by the name Application1.exe.config. You can create this file by using Visual Studio or by using Notepad.
3. Add the following XML to the file:

```xml
<?xml version="1.0" ?>
<configuration>
    <runtime>
        <assemblyBinding
            xmlns="urn:schemas-microsoft-com:asm.v1">
            <dependentAssembly>
                <assemblyIdentity
                    name="MathUtil"
                    publicKeyToken="d2ec12fd012cbcaf" />
                <bindingRedirect
                    oldVersion="1.0.0.0"
                    newVersion="1.1.0.0" />
            </dependentAssembly>
        </assemblyBinding>
    </runtime>
</configuration>
```

4. Right-click the Application1.exe file and select **Run as Administrator** to run the application. You'll need to run as administrator because the version 1.1 of the MathUtil assembly writes to the Windows event log, which requires elevated permissions.

5. Notice that a random number is displayed on the screen. The new version of the assembly creates an entry in the Windows event log. You can verify this by clicking **Start > Event Viewer** and then looking at the Application event log.

In this exercise, you created an application configuration file for Application1. The CLR will load this configuration file at the beginning of execution to configure the runtime behavior for the application. The `<assemblyBinding>` element specifies rules for binding to assemblies. This configuration file defines one rule that specifies that for an assembly with a particular identity, the CLR will redirect all requests for version 1.0.0.0 to version 1.1.0.0. The `publicKeyToken` that you specify here must be unique to the strong name that you generated. You can find out the `publicKeyToken` for your assembly by looking at the output of the `gacutil.exe` command when used with the /l option (as shown previously in this lesson).

Configuring a Publisher Policy

Publisher policy is an XML-based assembly created by the publisher of an assembly and released with an upgrade to set the policy on the assembly version that should be used.

Consider a scenario in which you ship the version 1.0 of the `MathUtil` shared assembly. After you ship, you discover a critical defect that must be resolved. You fix the defect and ship a new version of the `MathUtil` assembly versioned as 1.1. In this case, you would want to completely override all references to version 1.0 with version 1.1 for all the applications. One way to accomplish this is to modify the configuration for each application as shown in the previous exercise. However, that requires a lot of work and some applications might still accidentally refer to the defective assembly. A better solution is in the form of a publisher policy in which you do configuration changes only one time in the GAC. The following exercise shows you how to do this.

 CONFIGURE A PUBLISHER POLICY FOR AN ASSEMBLY

GET READY. To configure a publisher policy for an assembly, perform the following steps:

1. Navigate to the output folder of the MathUtil project.

2. Create a new public configuration file named policy.1.0.MathUtil.config. You can create this file by using Visual Studio or by using Notepad.

3. Add the following XML to the file. Be sure to change the `publicKeyToken` attribute to the value specific to your strong name:

```xml
<?xml version="1.0" ?>
<configuration>
    <runtime>
        <assemblyBinding
            xmlns="urn:schemas-microsoft-com:asm.v1">
            <dependentAssembly>
                <assemblyIdentity
                    name="MathUtil"
                    publicKeyToken="d2ec12fd012cbcaf" />
                <bindingRedirect
                    oldVersion="1.0.0.0"
                    newVersion="1.1.0.0" />
```

```
                </dependentAssembly>
            </assemblyBinding>
        </runtime>
</configuration>
```

4. Launch the Visual Studio command prompt as an administrator. Change the directory to the output folder for the MathUtil project.

5. Run the following command to invoke the assembly linker, which generates a publisher policy assembly as specified:

```
al.exe /link:policy.1.0.MathUtil.config
     /out:policy.1.0.MathUtil.dll
/keyfile:test.snk
```

6. Add the publisher policy assembly to the GAC by using the `gacutil` command:

```
gacutil.exe /i policy.1.0.MathUtil.dll
```

7. The publisher policy now overrides all references to MathUtil 1.0 with MathUtil 1.1. To verify this, navigate to the output folder of Application1 and delete the Application1.exe.config file to make sure that there is no application-specific configuration.

8. Run Application1.exe as an administrator. Notice that a random number is generated and an entry is written to the Windows Application event log. This verifies that the publisher policy is in-effect and version 1.1 of MathUtil is being used.

The name of the publisher policy assembly should be in a specific format: *policy.majorNumber.minorNumber.AssemblyName.dll*. Here, *majorNumber* is the major version number and *minorNumber* is the minor version number of the assembly that you want to override. *AssemblyName* is the name of the assembly. Once you create this publisher policy assembly, you'll need to install this new assembly in the GAC. Once you do that, the new binding policy will be applied to all references to version 1.0 of the `MathUtil` assembly on this particular computer. If the assembly is installed on multiple computers, you'll have to add the publisher policy assembly to the GAC of each computer.

SKILL SUMMARY

IN THIS LESSON, YOU LEARNED:

- The .NET Framework supports multiple programming languages. The language compilers that target the .NET Framework compile to a common intermediate language (CIL). The CIL is converted into the native code at runtime by the common language runtime (CLR) by using a process called just-in-time (JIT) compilation.
- The Common Language Infrastructure (CLI) is an international standard approved by ISO and Ecma International. The CLI standard provides the specifications for the executable code and the runtime environment in which the code runs.
- Common Type System (CTS) defines the rules for declaring, using, and managing data types and their operations. CTS helps with language integration and allows for objects written in one language to be used by objects written in another language as if they were written in the same language.
- Common Language Specification (CLS) defines the rules for programming language features. These are the rules that a language must comply with in order to interoperate with other CLS-compliant programming languages.
- The metadata is a structured way to represent information about a program structure that the CLI uses to locate and load classes at the runtime.

- Virtual Execution System (VES) specifies how the runtime loads and executes CLI-compatible programs. VES provides the services needed to execute code using the metadata to connect separately generated code at runtime. When the code is executed, the platform-specific VES compiles the CIL to the machine language according to the specific hardware and operating system.
- An assembly is a library of compiled code and is the fundamental unit of deployment, version control, and security configuration in the .NET Framework. Depending on how they are deployed, there are two types of assemblies: private and shared.
- A private assembly is local to the application that uses it and is deployed within the application's directory structure. Any changes to a private assembly cannot possibly affect any other installed application on the same machine. The .NET Framework does not impose any special versioning or naming requirements for a private assembly.
- A shared assembly is intended for use by multiple applications on a computer. Shared assemblies are signed with a strong name and are deployed to the global assembly cache.
- Strong name specifies an assembly's unique identity. Strong name is used to make sure that the applications can precisely refer to an assembly, thereby avoiding any conflicts in name, version, or publisher.
- The global assembly cache is the central repository for storing shared assemblies on a computer. The global assembly cache simplifies deployment by allowing multiple versions of an assembly to co-exist.
- Multiple versions of a shared assembly can co-exist in the global assembly cache. When you have multiple versions of an assembly installed in the global assembly cache, you can configure an application to use a specific version of the assembly.

■ Knowledge Assessment

Fill in the Blank

Complete the following sentences by writing the correct word or words in the blanks provided.

1. The _____ standard provides the specifications for the executable code and the runtime environment in which the code runs.

2. The _____ is a structured way to represent information about a program structure that the common language infrastructure uses to locate and load classes at the runtime.

3. The _____ specifies a set of rules that enables the code written in a programming language to interoperate with the code written in other programming languages.

4. A(n) _____ is a library of compiled code and is the fundamental unit of deployment, version control, and security configuration in the .NET Framework.

5. The _____ allows you to view the contents of an assembly (such as the manifest, metadata, and the common intermediate language code).

6. Shared assemblies are signed with a _____ and are deployed to the global assembly cache.

7. The _____ is the central repository for storing shared assemblies on a computer.

8. The _____ program can be used to add assemblies to the global assembly cache during development and testing.

9. The _____ program can be used to generate keys needed to create a strong name for an assembly.

10. The _____ of an assembly contains information such as version and identity of the assembly.

Multiple Choice

Circle the letter that corresponds to the best answer.

1. You work as a software developer for a large infrastructure company. You are writing a component that will be shared across several applications throughout the company. You want to place the assembly named CommonComponents.dll in the global assembly cache. You have already stored the company's public key in the assembly manifest for CommonComponents.dll. Which of the following commands should you run to accomplish your task?
   a. `sn.exe -Vr CommonComponents.dll`
   b. `sn.exe -Vu CommonComponents.dll`
   c. `gacutil.exe /i CommonComponents.dll`
   d. `gacutil.exe /u CommonComponents.dll`

2. You have written a component that will be shared among multiple applications. You want to prepare the component so that it can be added to the global assembly cache. You have assigned a version number and culture. Next, you want to add the public key information to the assembly manifest for the assembly. Which of the following tools should you use?
   a. sn.exe
   b. gacutil.exe
   c. installutil.exe
   d. al.exe

3. You have written a component that will be shared among multiple applications. You may have multiple versions of this component and each application that might use this component might refer to a specific version of the component. You need to make sure that applications can correctly use the component and you want to minimize deployment efforts. Where should you deploy this component?
   a. Store the component in the application folder for each application.
   b. Add the component to the global assembly cache.
   c. Add the component to the Windows System directory.
   d. Store the component anywhere that you like and specify the location by using the `<codebase>` element in the application configuration file.

4. Which of the following portions of the common language infrastructure defines the rules that a programming language must comply with in order to interoperate with other programming languages?
   a. Common Type System (CTS)
   b. Common Language Specification (CLS)
   c. metadata
   d. Virtual Execution System (VES)

5. Which of the following portions of the common language infrastructure defines the rules for declaring, using, and managing data types and their operations?
   a. Common Type System (CTS)
   b. Common Language Specification (CLS)
   c. metadata
   d. Virtual Execution System (VES)

6. You are working with a set of .NET Framework components that your application will use. You have access to the component assemblies but you don't have access to the

component's source code. You need to get information about the classes and methods provided in the assemblies. You decide to look into the assembly contents to look for this information. Which of the following sections of an assembly will give you the needed information?

a. Manifest

b. metadata

c. CIL code

d. resources

7. You have developed a new business application that helps users in entering sales orders. Some of the application's assemblies need to be added to the global assembly cache. The software application will be installed by the end-user. The installation process should be simple and similar to other applications on the user's computer. Which of the following solutions should you recommend?

a. Use the Windows Installer technology to install the application.

b. Use xcopy.exe for copying files to the Program folder and use gacutil.exe to copy the files to the global assembly cache.

c. Use installutil.exe for copying files to the Program folder and use gacutil.exe to copy the files to the global assembly cache.

d. Create a console application by using C# to copy the files to their correct locations.

8. You are responsible for maintaining the installation of a Windows application that processes orders. The application uses an assembly named CommonComponents. This assembly is signed with a strong name. You have installed version 1.0 of CommonComponents to the root directory of your Windows application. You later receive a version 2.0 of CommonComponents that you install to the global assembly cache, as well as the root directory of the application. You configure the application's configuration file to redirect calls to version 1.0 of CommonComponents with version 2.0. Finally, you receive version 3.0 of the CommonComponents assembly, which you install to the global assembly cache. At this time, you do not reconfigure the application configuration file. Now when you run the Windows application, which version of the CommonComponents assembly is loaded?

a. Version 1.0 from the application's root directory

b. Version 2.0 from the application's root directory

c. Version 2.0 from the global assembly cache

d. Version 3.0 from the global assembly cache

9. You ship the version 1.0 of the CommonComponents shared assembly. After you ship, you discover a critical defect that must be resolved. You fix the defect and ship a new version (1.1) of the CommonComponents assembly. You want to completely override all references to version 1.0 with version 1.1 for all the applications that use the CommonComponents assembly on a computer. The solution you suggest must minimize the deployment and configuration efforts. What should you do?

a. Modify the application configuration file for each application that uses the CommonComponents assembly with the following:

```xml
<?xml version="1.0" ?>
<configuration>
    <runtime>
        <assemblyBinding
            xmlns="urn:schemas-microsoft-com:asm.v1">
            <dependentAssembly>
                <assemblyIdentity
                    name=" CommonComponents"
                    publicKeyToken="e3ec12fd024dccae" />
                <bindingRedirect
```

```
oldVersion="1.0.0.0"
newVersion="1.1.0.0" />
</dependentAssembly>
</assemblyBinding>
</runtime>
</configuration>
```

b. Modify the application configuration file for each application that uses the CommonComponents assembly with the following:

```
<?xml version="1.0" ?>
<configuration>
    <runtime>
        <assemblyBinding
            xmlns="urn:schemas-microsoft-com:asm.v1">
            <dependentAssembly>
                <assemblyIdentity
                    name=" CommonComponents"
                    publicKeyToken="e3ec12fd024dccae" />
                <bindingRedirect
                    oldVersion="1.1.0.0"
                    newVersion="1.0.0.0" />
            </dependentAssembly>
        </assemblyBinding>
    </runtime>
</configuration>
```

c. Create a publisher policy file for the CommonComponents assembly with the following XML. Convert the XML file to a publisher policy DLL.

```
<?xml version="1.0" ?>
<configuration>
    <runtime>
        <assemblyBinding
            xmlns="urn:schemas-microsoft-com:asm.v1">
            <dependentAssembly>
                <assemblyIdentity
                    name=" CommonComponents"
                    publicKeyToken="e3ec12fd024dccae" />
                <bindingRedirect
                    oldVersion="1.0.0.0"
                    newVersion="1.1.0.0" />
            </dependentAssembly>
        </assemblyBinding>
    </runtime>
</configuration>
```

d. Create a publisher policy file for the CommonComponents assembly with the following XML. Convert the XML file to a publisher policy DLL.

```
<?xml version="1.0" ?>
<configuration>
    <runtime>
        <assemblyBinding
            xmlns="urn:schemas-microsoft-com:asm.v1">
            <dependentAssembly>
                <assemblyIdentity
```

```
                                 name=" CommonComponents"
                                 publicKeyToken="e3ec12fd024dccae" />
                            <bindingRedirect
                                 oldVersion="1.1.0.0"
                                 newVersion="1.0.0.0" />
                       </dependentAssembly>
                  </assemblyBinding>
            </runtime>
      </configuration>
```

10. You create a new shared code library, CommonComponent.dll. You also install the corresponding assembly, CommonComponents, to the global assembly cache. You now need to uninstall the assembly from the global assembly cache. Which of the following commands should you use?
    a. `gacutil /i MathUtil.dll`
    b. `gacutil /l MathUtil`
    c. `gacutil /u MathUtil.dll`
    d. `gacutil /u MathUtil`

■ Competency Assessment

Project 4-1: Looking at an Assembly Manifest

Your team is developing code that uses assemblies developed by other companies. You have access to a code library in GraphTools.dll but you do not have access to the source code. You need to find the version of the assembly to make sure that you use the correct version. How should you verify the version of the assembly?

Project 4-2: Uninstalling an Assembly from the Global Assembly Cache

Your team is developing code that is compiled into the vcsComponents.dll file. The name of this culture-neutral assembly is **VcsComponents** and its public key token is a3db12fd012cbdbe. You install version 1.0 and version 1.1 of this assembly to the global assembly cache. You now need to uninstall only the version 1.0 of the assembly from the GAC. What should you do?

■ Proficiency Assessment

Project 4-3: Using Multiple Languages

You are writing code for an application that uses functionality from other reusable assemblies. Your application's code is written in Visual Basic. The application uses an assembly, MathUtil, which was compiled by using a C# compiler. How would you write code that calls the code written in a different .NET Framework programming language? (For this project, you can use the MathUtil C# library project that you created earlier in this lesson.)

Project 4-4: Delay Sign an Assembly

Your team is developing code that will be deployed as shared assembly. Multiple programmers are involved in developing the code. The code for the shared assembly is compiled into a file named vcsComponents.dll. This code needs to be signed with a strong name so that it can be deployed to the global assembly cache for development and testing. You need to limit access to the private key. The key-pair file keyfile.snk contains both public and private keys. What steps should you take to add the vcsComponents.dll file to the global assembly cache?

Understanding Input/ Output (I/O) Classes

EXAM OBJECTIVE MATRIX

SKILLS/CONCEPTS	MTA EXAM OBJECTIVE	MTA EXAM OBJECTIVE NUMBER
Understanding Console Input/Output (I/O)	Understand console I/O.	4.2
Understanding .NET File Classes in the .NET Framework	Understand .NET file classes.	4.1
Understanding XML Classes in the .NET Framework	Understand XML classes in the .NET Framework.	4.3

KEY TERMS

attribute

backing store

binary file

command-line arguments

command piping

console applications

element

stream

text files

XML

XML schema

You are a software developer for the Northwind Corporation. As part of your work, you interact with and process data about customers, products, suppliers, and orders. The applications that you develop need to input and output data in different formats, including text, binary, and XML. You will also need to read data from and write data to the console window. To be effective at your work, you also need to know how to work with the console, the file system, and the XML-formatted data.

■ Understanding Console Input/Output (I/O)

THE BOTTOM LINE

Console applications do not have a graphical user interface and use a text-mode console window to interact with the user. Console-based applications are best suited for tasks that require minimal or no user interface.

CERTIFICATION READY
What is a console application?
4.2

A console application is a program designed to be used via a text-based interface. A commonly used console application in Windows is the command window (cmd.exe). Each console application has an associated input stream that maintains a queue of input events, such as keystrokes. Each console application also has an associated output stream, which is used to display the output messages.

Console applications can interactively read characters from the console window and can also get input via the command-line parameters. The output of the console application is written to the console window.

A console application is best suited for tasks that require minimal or no user interface. Think of these applications as commands. You issue the command on the command line (optionally passing a parameter) and the application accomplishes the specified task and optionally displays a message summarizing the action. Console applications can also be chained by taking advantage of the command piping provided by Windows. With **command piping**, you can pass the output of a command as an input to another command, thereby creating more powerful commands by combining simple commands.

Occasionally, GUI-based applications might also want to interact with the console. For example, if a Windows-based application encounters a fault at runtime and fails to create the user interface, the application might resort to displaying messages on a console window that might help a user or an administrator troubleshoot the fault.

TAKE NOTE *

To enable reading from or writing to the console from a Windows Forms application, set the project's Output Type to Console Application in the project's properties.

Using the Console Class

In this section, you'll learn how to use the System.Console class for input and output in a console application.

The `Console` class in the System namespace provides methods to interact with the console window. Table 5-1 lists some of the methods of the `Console` class that helps you read data from and write data to the console window.

Table 5-1

Methods available to read data from and write data to the console window

METHOD NAME	DESCRIPTION
Read	Reads the next character from the input stream as an integer. If there are no more characters to be read, a negative one (-1) is returned. The return type of the Read method is an int but you can convert the return value to the Char struct by using the Convert.ToChar() method. The Char struct provides several methods for working with character data. An example is the Char.IsLetter() method which checks if a given letter is a letter or not.
ReadKey	Reads the next character or function key pressed by the user as `ConsoleKeyInfo`.
ReadLine	Reads the next line of characters from the input stream as a string.
Write	Writes text to the output stream
WriteLine	Writes text to the output stream, followed by the line terminator character.

Visual Studio provides a Console Application template, as you have seen in the previous lessons, to quickly create a console application. The following exercise shows you how to use the methods of the `Console` class for input and output.

CREATE A CONSOLE APPLICATION

GET READY. Launch Microsoft Visual Studio and then perform the following steps:

1. Create a new project based on the Console Application template (see Figure 5-1). Name the project as ConsoleIO.

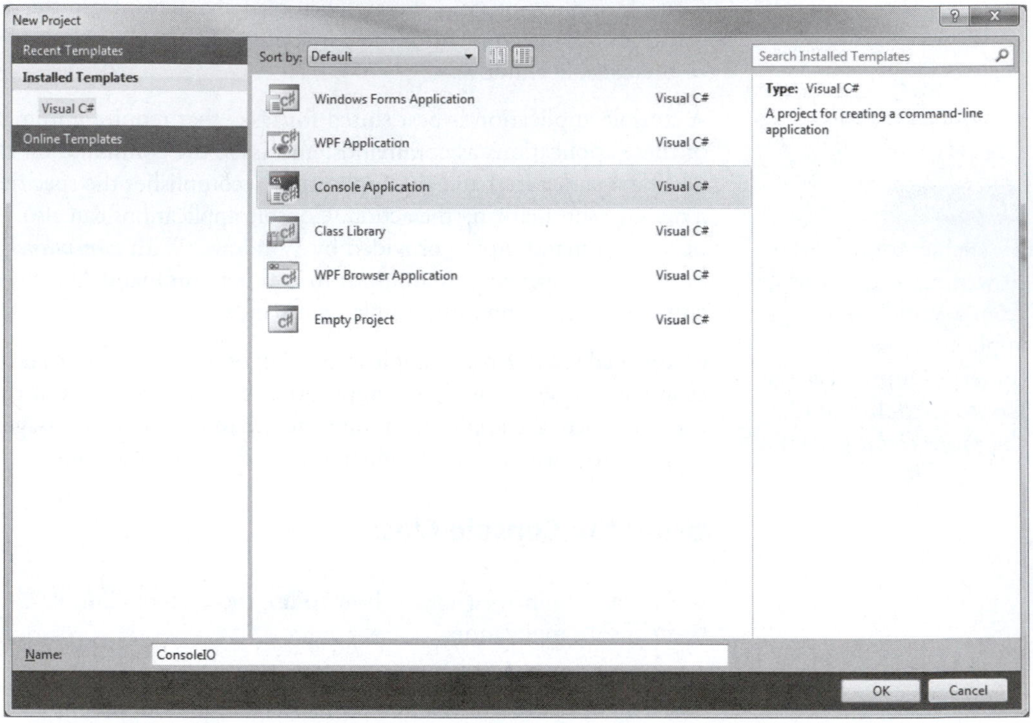

Figure 5-1

The Console Application template

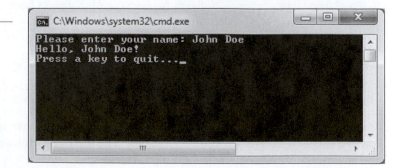

2. In the Program.cs file, modify the code for the Main method as follows:

```csharp
static void Main(string[] args)
{
    Console.Write("Please enter your name: ");
    string name = Console.ReadLine();
    Console.WriteLine("Hello, {0}!", name);
    Console.Beep();

    Console.Write("Press a key to quit...");
    Console.ReadKey();
}
```

3. Click **Debug > Start Debugging** (or press **F5**) to run the program. A console window displays (see Figure 5-2).

Figure 5-2

The Console Application window

4. Type a name and press **Enter**. A greeting is displayed, followed by a beep from computer speakers. Next, the console window awaits any keystroke from you before the application exits.

Working with Command-line Arguments

> In this section, you'll learn how to accept command-line parameters into a console application.

In the previous exercise, the console application ran in an interactive mode. That is, when the application started, it waited for input from the user and then processed that input. At times, you might want to pass the input as part of the command line so that the application can start processing the input without waiting. This is especially useful when console applications are run as commands in a batch file.

The `Main` method is the entry point to a console application. The ***command-line arguments*** are the values passed to the `Main` method from the operating system. If you need to pass more than one argument, you can separate the arguments by space. The `Main` method receives the command-line arguments as a string array.

The following exercise shows you how to create a console application that accepts a list of numbers as a command-line argument and displays the square root of the numbers. Since there is not a square root operator, the `System.Math` class is available to provide some more advanced mathematical behavior.

⊙ PROCESS COMMAND-LINE ARGUMENTS

GET READY. To process the command-line arguments from a console application, perform the following steps:

1. Create a new project based on the Console Application template. Name the project as SquareRoots. This application calculates the square roots of the numbers passed as command-line arguments.

2. In the Program.cs file, modify the code inside the `Main` method as follows:

```
static void Main(string[] args)
{
    foreach (string item in args)
    {
        double number = Convert.ToDouble(item);
        double squareRoot =
            Math.Round(Math.Sqrt(number), 2);
        Console.WriteLine(squareRoot);
    }
}
```

3. Click **Build > Build Solution** (or press **F6**) to build the project.

4. Open a command prompt and then navigate to the path of the project's .exe file (the executable is created by default in the bin\debug or the bin\release folder under the project's folder).

5. Execute the following command:

```
SquareRoots 100 200 300
```

You'll see that the command calculates and displays the square root of the given numbers in the command window.

6. Alternatively, you can also pass the command-line argument from within Visual Studio by using the project's properties window (see Figure 5-3). To view the project's properties window, click **Project > SquareRoots Properties** and then select the **Debug** tab.

Figure 5-3

Setting command-line arguments in the project's properties window

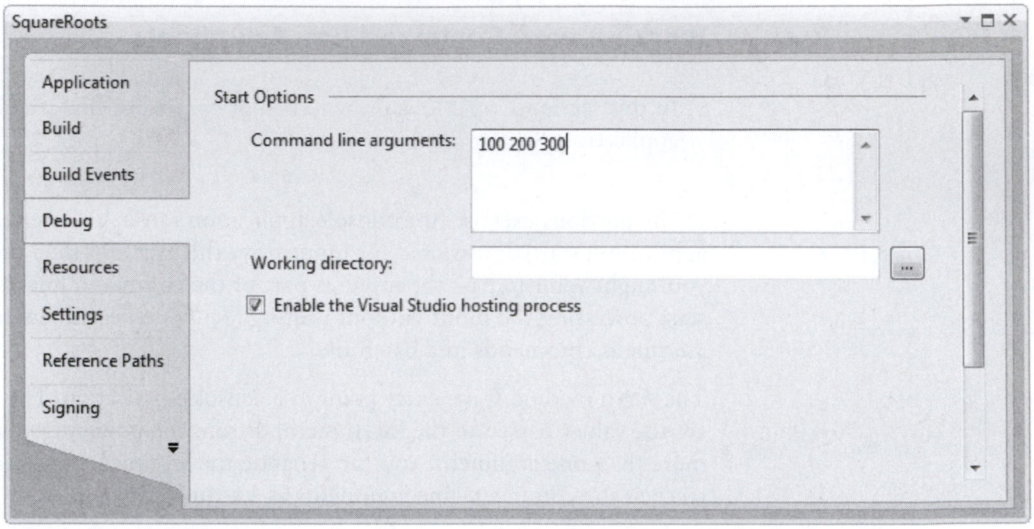

7. Click **Project > Set as StartUp Project** to set the project as the startup project.
8. Press **Ctrl+F5** to run the program without debugging. This command pauses the program so that you get a chance to review the output before the program ends.

■ Understanding .NET File Classes in the .NET Framework

↓ **THE BOTTOM LINE**

Business applications might need to work with data stored in files. You might need to read and write text or binary data. You might also need to perform file operations such as copying, moving, or deleting a file. The .NET Framework provides the classes for file-based input and output as part of the System.IO namespace.

CERTIFICATION READY
What is a backing store?
4.1

File-based input and output in the .NET Framework revolves around the concept of streams and a backing store. A **stream** represents a flow of raw data. A **backing store** represents the source or destination of the stream. A backing store might be anything, such as a disk file, memory, network connection, and so on. You find classes for working with streams and backing stores in the System.IO namespace.

Files can have data either in plain-text format or in binary format. **Text files** are the data files that contain only character-based data. These files are often organized as lines of text separated by end-of-line characters. The StreamReader and the StreamWriter classes provide you with an easy way to manipulate such text files.

Binary files store content as a sequence of bytes. Although binary files cannot be read by humans (like text files), they are capable of storing a different variety of data, such as images, sounds, video, and so on. You need a computer program in order to interpret the contents of a binary file. The BinaryReader and the BinaryWriter classes provide you with an easy way to manipulate binary files.

Table 5-2 lists select classes from the System.IO namespace.

Table 5-2

Select classes from the System.IO namespace

Class Name	Description
BinaryReader	Reads bytes from the underlying stream and advances the current position of the stream.
BinaryWriter	Writes bytes to the underlying stream and advances the current position of the stream.
Directory	Provides static methods to work (creating, deleting, moving, enumerating) with directories.
DirectoryInfo	Provides instant methods to work (creating, deleting, moving, enumerating) with directories.
File	Provides static methods to work (creating, deleting, moving, copying, opening) with files. Also helps in the creation of FileStream objects.
FileInfo	Provides instant methods to work (creating, deleting, moving, copying, opening) with files. Also helps in the creation of FileStream objects.
FileStream	Provides a stream whose backing store is a file. Supports read and write operations.
MemoryStream	Provides a stream whose backing store is memory. Supports read and write operations.
StreamReader	A reader that can read the next character (in the specified encoding) from the stream and advances the stream by one character.
StreamWriter	Writes characters (in the specified encoding) to the stream.
StringReader	A reader that can read from a string and advances the stream by one character.
StringWriter	A writer that can write a string using an underlying StringBuilder.

Understanding File Operations

The File and FileInfo classes provide methods for working with the disk files. The File and the FileInfo classes in the System.IO namespace allow you to manipulate disk files. These classes provide methods to help you do file operations such as copy, move, or delete. The File class contains only static methods while the FileInfo class contains instance methods with similar names.

The static methods of the File class perform security checks each time they are called. So, if you are going to perform multiple operations on a file, it might be more efficient to use the methods in the FieInfo class instead of the File class. In contrast, if security if paramount then it might be helpful to use the File class methods.

The following exercise demonstrates how to use the methods in the File class.

➡ MANIPULATE DISK FILES

GET READY. To manipulate disk files, perform the following steps:

1. Create a new project based on the Console Application template. Name the project as FileOperations.

2. In the Program.cs file, modify the code inside the Main method as follows:

```
static void Main(string[] args)
{
    // Copying a file
    File.Copy(@"..\..\Program.cs", "Program.txt");
    // Display file contents
    string programText =
        File.ReadAllText("Program.txt");
    Console.WriteLine(programText);
    // Delete a file
    File.Delete("Program.txt");
    // check if a file exists
    if (!File.Exists("Program.txt"))
        Console.WriteLine(
        "Program.txt was successfully deleted");
}
```

3. Add the following using directive to your code:

```
using System.IO;
```

4. Click **Project > Set as StartUp Project** to set the project as the startup project.

5. Build and run the program (press **Ctrl+F5**) and then review the messages in the console window.

TAKE NOTE ✱

Characters such as \ have special meaning when included in a string. These characters are called an escape character. When you want to treat these characters as plain text, you can escape the character by prefixing it with a back slash (\). When you use the symbol @ to quote the string, all the escape characters in the string are treated as plain text.

The code in this exercise first copies the program's source file (Program.cs) to the project's output directory as Program.txt. Next, the text in the file is displayed to the console window. Subsequently, the newly created file, Program.txt, is deleted. Finally, the program checks if the Program.txt file still exists and displays a message if the file does not exist.

Reading and Writing Text Files

> The `StreamReader` and `StreamWriter` classes provide methods to respectively read data from and write data to text files.

A text file is a disk file that stores only character-based data. Each character can be represented by a sequence of bit patterns. Character encoding describes the rules by which each character is represented. There are different encoding schemes available in the .NET framework, such as ASCIIEncoding, UTF8Encoding, and UnicodeEncoding.

TAKE NOTE ✱

It is important to make sure that you use the same encoding scheme for reading and writing data. If you use a different coding scheme than what is expected, the text might be garbled.

Each encoding scheme stores characters in different ways. For example, the ASCIIEncoding uses a 7-bit pattern to represent each character while UTF8Encoding is a variable width encoding where each character is represented by using one to four bytes. The more bits you use, the more characters you can represent. With seven bits, ASCIIEncoding can only represent a limited set of 128 unique characters. However, by using UTF8Encoding, you can represent characters not only from the English alphabet but from all the other international languages.

The StreamReader and StreamWriter classes provide methods to read data from and write data to text files using the specified encoding. Unless specified otherwise, both classes default to using UTF8Encoding.

The following exercise demonstrates how to use the StreamWriter and the StreamReader file classes.

⊕ USE READ AND WRITE TEXT FILES

GET READY. To read and write text files, perform the following steps:

1. Create a new project based on the Console Application template. Name the project as TextFiles.

2. In the Program.cs file, modify the code inside the Program class as follows:

```csharp
static void Main(string[] args)
{
    string fileName = "fileList.txt";
    WriteTextFile(fileName);
    ReadTextFile(fileName);
}

static void WriteTextFile(string fileName)
{
    try
    {
        // DirectoryInfo takes a string with the file
        // path as a parameter
        DirectoryInfo dInfo = new DirectoryInfo(
            Environment.GetFolderPath(
            Environment.SpecialFolder.MyDocuments));
        StringBuilder sb = new StringBuilder();
        foreach (FileInfo fileInfo in dInfo.GetFiles())
        {
            sb.AppendLine(fileInfo.Name);
        }

        using (StreamWriter sw =
            new StreamWriter(fileName))
        {
            sw.Write(sb.ToString());
        }
    }
    catch (Exception ex)
    {
        Console.WriteLine("Error: {0}", ex.Message);
    }}

static void ReadTextFile(string fileName)
{
    try
    {
        using (StreamReader sr =
            new StreamReader(fileName))
```

```
        {
            string line;
            while ((line = sr.ReadLine()) != null)
            {
                Console.WriteLine(line);
            }
        }
    }
    catch (Exception ex)
    {
        Console.WriteLine("Error: {0}", ex.Message);
    }
}
```

3. Add the following using directive to your code:

   using System.IO;

4. Click **Project > Set as StartUp Project** to set the project as the startup project.

5. Build and run the program (press **Ctrl+F5**) and then review the output in the console window.

The StreamWriter constructor accepts the name of the file, or a stream that you wish to write to. You can also specify the encoding that you would like to use. In this exercise, encoding is not specified, so it defaults to UTF8Encoding. When the StreamWriter object is ready, you can call the Write method to write contents to the text file.

Similarly, to read from a text file, you first create an instance of the StreamReader class. Just as in the StreamWriter constructor, you can specify the file name and the encoding in the StreamReader constructor. Always make sure that you use the same encoding for reading from and writing to a file. There are several methods available for reading the text. You can read a character, a block of characters, a line of characters, or all the contents of a file.

The StreamWriter and StreamReader objects open unmanaged operating system resources, such as file handles. When you are done using these objects in your code, you should call the Dispose method so that the unmanaged resources are correctly disposed. A good practice is to use the StreamWriter and StreamReader object in a using statement as shown in the previous exercise. The using statement automatically calls the Dispose method for you. The using statement works only with objects that implement the IDisposable interface.

The text files contain plain text. That is, you can open a text file in any text editor (such as Notepad or Visual Studio) and view or edit its contents.

Reading and Writing Binary Files

The BinaryReader and BinaryWriter classes provide methods to respectively read data from and write data to binary files.

A *binary file* is a disk file that can store any type of data. Examples of binary data include mathematical data, image data, video data, audio data, or a combination of them all.

To write to a file, you first create an instance of the BinaryWriter class. The BinaryWriter constructor accepts a stream that you wish to write to. You can create a file stream by calling the File.Open method. The File.Open method takes the file name and a parameter of type FileMode (examples of FileMode value include Create, Open, Append) to tell the operating system how to open the file. When the `BinaryWriter` object is ready, you can call the `Write` method to write contents to the binary file.

Similarly, to read from a binary file, you first create an instance of the `BinaryReader` class. The `BinaryReader` class provides several methods for reading; each is designed for reading a specific type of data.

The `BinaryWriter` and `BinaryReader` objects open unmanaged operating system resources, such as file handles. When you are done using these objects in your code, you should call the `Dispose` method so that the unmanaged resources are correctly disposed. You can also use the `using` statement as shown in the previous exercise. The `using` statement automatically calls the `Dispose` method for you.

The following exercise shows you how to write data to a binary file and read data from a binary file.

 WRITE DATA TO A BINARY FILE AND READ DATA FROM A BINARY FILE

GET READY. To read and write binary files, perform the following steps:

1. Create a new project based on the Console Application template. Name the project as BinaryFiles.

2. In the Program.cs file, modify the code inside the `Program` class as follows:

```csharp
static void Main(string[] args)
{
    string fileName = "data.bin";

    WriteBinaryFile(fileName);
    ReadBinaryFile(fileName);
}

static void WriteBinaryFile(string fileName)
{
    Int32 int32Data = 5;
    string stringData = "Sample String";
    Single singleData = 3.141f;
    bool boolData = true;

    using (BinaryWriter writer =
        new BinaryWriter(
        File.Open(fileName, FileMode.Create)))
    {
        writer.Write(int32Data);
        writer.Write(stringData);
        writer.Write(singleData);
        writer.Write(boolData);
    }
}

static void ReadBinaryFile(string fileName)
{
    if (File.Exists(fileName))
    {
        using (BinaryReader reader =
            new BinaryReader(
            File.Open(fileName, FileMode.Open)))
```

```
        {
            Console.WriteLine(reader.ReadInt32());
            Console.WriteLine(reader.ReadString());
            Console.WriteLine(reader.ReadSingle());
            Console.WriteLine(reader.ReadBoolean());
        }
    }
}
```

3. Add the following using directive to your code:

   using System.IO;

4. Click **Project > Set as StartUp Project** to set the project as the startup project.

5. Build and run the program (press **Ctrl+F5**) and then review the output in the console window.

This exercise writes four types of data to the binary file:

- An integer
- A string
- A floating point number
- A Boolean value

The order in which you read or write binary data is important. If you try to read a floating point number from a disk when the actual data stored is a string, you will get unexpected results.

The Write method of the BinaryWriter class provides several overrides to accommodate different data types. However, for BinaryReader (the return types are different for each read method), there are separate read methods, one for each data type.

The binary files contain binary data. You won't be able to read binary data using a plain text editor such as Notepad. Only programs that know how to decode the binary data will be able to read the binary files.

■ Understanding XML Classes in the .NET Framework

↓
THE BOTTOM LINE

XML (Extensible Markup Language) is a text-based format for representing structured data. As a business software developer, you must know how to work with XML because XML is widely used in applications that exchange information between organizations, Web site publishing, object serialization, remote procedure calls, and so on.

CERTIFICATION READY
What is XML?
4.3

XML is a markup language developed by the World Wide Web Consortium (W3C). XML files contain data and metadata (information about the data stored). Data and metadata are stored in human readable format.

Similar to HTML (Hypertext Markup Language), XML uses tags to describe data. However, unlike HTML, the tags are not pre-defined. You can create your own tags depending on your application's need. For example, for storing a customer record, you can create tags such as Id, Name, Phone and so on.

Here's a concrete example to start with. This XML file represents data for two customers:

```
<?xml version="1.0" encoding="utf-8"?>
<!--Customer List-->
<Customers>
    <Customer Id="ALFKI">
        <CompanyName>Alfreds Futterkiste</CompanyName>
        <Phone>030-0074321</Phone>
    </Customer>
    <Customer Id="EASTC">
        <CompanyName>Eastern Connection</CompanyName>
        <Phone>(171) 555-0297</Phone>
    </Customer>
</Customers>
```

Even without knowing much about XML, you can understand the contents of this file just by looking at them. XML consists of tags (contained within angular brackets) and data. Tags always appear in pairs, with each opening tag matched by a closing tag (For example, `<Customers>` is an opening tag and `</Customers>` is a closing tag).

The first line of an XML document is the following XML declaration:

```
<?xml version="1.0" encoding="utf-8"?>
```

The XML tags that begin with the `<?` characters are called processing instructions. The `<?xml` processing instruction tells us that the document is an XML document, conforms to the XML version 1.0 specifications, and uses UTF-8 character set for its data elements.

An opening tag and closing tag together with their content is called an ***element***. For example, here is a single XML element from the aforementioned document:

```
<Phone>030-0074321</Phone>
```

This defines an element with the name `Phone` whose value is `030-0074321`. Elements can be nested but they cannot overlap. For example, the following XML is invalid because of the overlap between the `CompanyName` element and the `Phone` element.

```
<Customer Id="EASTC">
        <CompanyName>Eastern Connection<Phone>
        </Phone>(171) 555-0297</CompanyName>
    </Customer>
</Customers>
```

XML documents are hierarchical in nature. Every XML document contains a single root element that contains all the other nodes. An XML document can be visualized as a tree of nodes as shown in Figure 5-4.

Elements can contain attributes. An attribute is placed inside the opening tag of the element. An ***attribute*** is a piece of data that further describes an element, as follows:

```
<Customer Id="ALFKI">
```

Here, the `Customer` element includes an attribute whose name is `Id` and whose value is `ALFKI`.

Finally, an XML document can contain comments. Comments start with the characters `<!--` and end with the characters `-->`.

Figure 5-4

Hierarchical view of an XML document

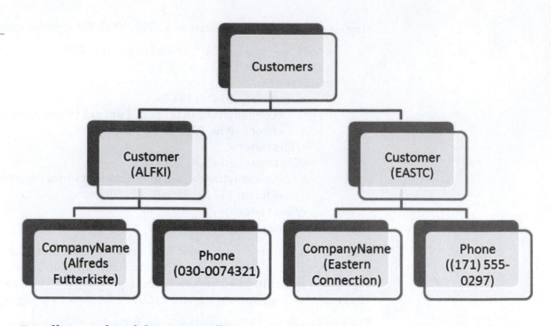

Reading and Writing XML Files

The XmlReader and XmlWriter classes provide methods to respectively read data from and write data to XML files.

There are many ways in which you can work with XML data. The classes to work with XML data are organized in the System.Xml namespace. This section focuses on the XmlReader and XmlWriter classes. These classes provide a fast, non-cached, and forward-only way to read or write XML data.

In the following exercise, you learn how to use XmlReader and XmlWriter to read and write XML data to a file named Customers.xml.

READ AND WRITE AN XML FILE

GET READY. To read and write XML files, perform the following steps:

1. Create a new console application project named XmlReadWrite.
2. Add the following code to the Main method of the Program class:

```
static void Main(string[] args)
{
    string fileName = "Customers.xml";
    WriteXmlFile(fileName);
    ReadXmlFile(fileName);
}

static void WriteXmlFile(string fileName)
{
    XmlWriterSettings settings =
    new XmlWriterSettings();
        settings.Indent = true;
        settings.IndentChars = " ";
        settings.NewLineOnAttributes = true;

    using (XmlWriter writer =
        XmlWriter.Create(fileName, settings))
    {
```

```
        writer.WriteComment("Customer List");
        writer.WriteStartElement("Customers");
        writer.WriteStartElement("Customer");
        writer.WriteAttributeString("Id", "ALFKI");
        writer.WriteElementString(
            "CompanyName", "Alfreds Futterkiste");
        writer.WriteElementString(
            "Phone", "030-0074321");
        writer.WriteEndElement();
        writer.WriteStartElement("Customer");
        writer.WriteAttributeString("Id", "EASTC");
        writer.WriteElementString(
            "CompanyName", "Eastern Connection");
        writer.WriteElementString(
            "Phone", "(171) 555-0297");
        writer.WriteEndElement();
        writer.WriteEndElement();
        writer.Flush();
    }
}
static void ReadXmlFile(string fileName)
{
    using (XmlReader reader =
        XmlReader.Create(fileName))
    {
        while (reader.Read())
        {
            if (reader.IsStartElement())
            {
                switch (reader.Name)
                {
                    case "CompanyName":
                        if (reader.Read())
                            Console.Write(
                            "Company Name: {0}, ",
                            reader.Value);
                        break;
                    case "Phone":
                        if (reader.Read())
                            Console.WriteLine(
                        "Phone: {0}", reader.Value);
                        break;
                }
            }
        }
    }
}
```

3. Add the following using directive to the program:

   using System.Xml;

4. Build and run the program (press **Ctrl+F5**). You'll see a list of all the company names and their phone numbers in the console window.

The code in this exercise creates a new instance of the XmlWriter class as part of the WriteXmlFile method. The XmlWriter class provides methods to write XML comments, elements, attributes, and data. The `XmlSettings` class controls settings such as indentation. The method creates the following XML data in the Customers.xml file:

```
<?xml version="1.0" encoding="utf-8"?>
<!--Customer List-->
<Customers>
    <Customer Id="ALFKI">
        <CompanyName>Alfreds Futterkiste</CompanyName>
        <Phone>030-0074321</Phone>
    </Customer>
    <Customer Id="EASTC">
        <CompanyName>Eastern Connection</CompanyName>
        <Phone>(171) 555-0297</Phone>
    </Customer>
</Customers>
```

The next part of the program reads the XML data stored in the customers.xml file by using the `XmlReader` class. You create an instance of the `XmlReader` class by using the `XmlReader.Create` method. This method will throw an exception if the file is not found. This `ReadXmlFile` method will terminate when `XmlReader.Read` method has nothing to read. You can use properties of `XmlReader` (such as `Name` and `Value`) to access various portions of XML.

Understanding XML Schema

XML schema describes the structure of an XML document. An XML document is considered valid only when it conforms to its XML schema.

Any XML file that conforms to the syntactical rules for XML is considered well formed. However, that does not automatically render the file valid. When an XML file conforms to a predefined schema, the file is considered to be valid. The XML Schema is also specified in the XML format and can be present in the same file as data or can be specified in a separate file. In this section, you will learn how to create an XML schema and how to validate an XML data file against a specified schema.

XML schema is particularly important when an XML file is used to share data between two applications. Without XML schema, the applications won't know how the data in the XML file is structured. If you already have a well-formed and well-structured XML data file, you can infer XML schema from the XML data by using the .NET Framework XML Schema Tool (xsd.exe). The following exercise shows you how to do this.

⊙ USE THE XML SCHEMA DEFINITION TOOL (XSD.EXE)

GET READY. To use the XML schema definition tool, perform the following steps:

1. Create a new console application project named XmlSchema.
2. Copy the Customers.xml file that was created in the previous exercise and paste it to the output path of the XmlSchema project.
3. Click **Start > Visual Studio 2010 > Visual Studio Tools > Visual Studio Command Prompt**.
4. Switch the path to the project output folder and then run the following command:

   ```
   xsd.exe Customers.xml
   ```

   Notice that the tool generates a new file by the name of Customers.xsd with the following content. This file specifies the XML schema. As you can notice in the schema, the <xs:element> tag specifies the name and type of the XML element, the <xs:attribute> tag specify the attribute names and its corresponding type:

```
<?xml version="1.0" encoding="utf-8"?>
<xs:schema id="Customers"
    xmlns=""
    xmlns:xs="http://www.w3.org/2001/XMLSchema"
    xmlns:msdata="urn:schemas-microsoft-com:xml-msdata">
    <xs:element name="Customers"
        msdata:IsDataSet="true"
        msdata:UseCurrentLocale="true">
    <xs:complexType>
        <xs:choice minOccurs="0" maxOccurs="unbounded">
            <xs:element name="Customer">
                <xs:complexType>
                    <xs:sequence>
                        <xs:element name="CompanyName"
                            type="xs:string"
                            minOccurs="0" msdata:Ordinal="0" />
                        <xs:element name="Phone"
                            type="xs:string"
                            minOccurs="0" msdata:Ordinal="1" />
                    </xs:sequence>
                        <xs:attribute name="Id"
                            type="xs:string" />
                </xs:complexType>
            </xs:element>
        </xs:choice>
    </xs:complexType>
</xs:element>
</xs:schema>
```

As a result of this exercise, you generated a schema file by inferring schema from an XML data file. In the next exercise, you'll learn how to validate a XML data file against a schema file.

➡ VALIDATE XML SCHEMA

GET READY. To validate XML schema, perform the following steps:

1. Open the Console Application project XmlSchema that you created in the previous exercise.

2. Add the following code to the Program class:

```
static void Main(string[] args)
{
    // Create a cache of schema to validate against
    XmlSchemaSet schemaSet = new XmlSchemaSet();
    // when null, use the targetNamespace
    // specified in the schema.
    schemaSet.Add(null, "Customers.xsd");

    // Define the validation rules
    XmlReaderSettings settings =
        new XmlReaderSettings();
    settings.Schemas = schemaSet;
    settings.ConformanceLevel =
        ConformanceLevel.Document;
```

```
            settings.ValidationType = ValidationType.Schema;
            settings.ValidationFlags =

        // Use the ValidationEventHandler delegate to define
        // the response to validation
        XmlSchemaValidationFlags.ReportValidationWarnings;
            settings.ValidationEventHandler +=
                new ValidationEventHandler(
                settings_ValidationEventHandler);

            using (XmlReader reader =
                XmlReader.Create("Customers.xml", settings))
            {
                while (reader.Read());
            }
        }

        static void settings_ValidationEventHandler(
            object sender, ValidationEventArgs e)
        {
            Console.WriteLine(e.Message);
        }
```

Add the following using directive to the program:

```
using System.Xml;
using System.Xml.Schema;
```

3. Build and run the program (press **Ctrl+F5**). On the first run, you will not get any messages in the console window because the XML data conforms to the schema.

4. Modify the Customers.xml file and change the CustomerName tag to Customer. Be sure to change the matching closing tag as well. At this point, the XML is still well formed but it is invalid because it doesn't conform to the schema. The schema requires the name of the XML tag to be CustomerName rather than Customer.

5. Run the program again. The following validation error is displayed in the console window:

```
The element 'Customer' has invalid child element 'Company'. List
of possible elements expected: 'CompanyName, Phone'.
```

In this exercise, you first created an XmlSchemaSet object in which you specify the location of the XML schema file. Next, you create an XmlReaderSettings object and you set the ValidationType property as ValidationType.Schema to indicate that you would like to validate the XML data on the specified schema. Next, you attach an event handler on the ValidationEventHandler event to get notification when any validation errors are encountered.

Finally, you read the XML data file by using XmlReader. The XmlReader object receives validation settings as a parameter to its Create method. The constructor for the XmlReader class is protected and the class is **abstract**. We use the Create method as a mechanism for creating a reference to something that inherits from XmlReader class based on the parameters that are passed in. As the file is being read, XmlReader also performs schema validation and raises the ValidationEventHandler event when an error is encountered.

SKILL SUMMARY

IN THIS LESSON YOU LEARNED:

- Console applications do not have a graphical user interface; they use a text-mode console window to interact with the user. Console-based applications are best suited for tasks that require minimal or no user interface. The `Console` class in the System namespace provides methods to interact with the console window.
- The `File` and `FileInfo` classes in the System.IO namespace provide methods for working with the disk files.
- A text file is a disk file that stores only character-based data. The `StreamReader` and `StreamWriter` classes provide methods to respectively read data from and write data to text files.
- A binary file is a disk file that can store any type of data. Examples of binary data include mathematical data, image data, video data, audio data, or a combination of them all. The `BinaryReader` and `BinaryWriter` classes provide methods to respectively read data from and write data to binary files.
- XML is a text-based format for representing structured data. There are many ways to work with XML data. The classes to work with XML data are organized in the System.Xml namespace. The `XmlReader` and `XmlWriter` classes provide methods to respectively read data from and write data to XML files.

■ Knowledge Assessment

Fill in the Blank

Complete the following sentences by writing the correct word or words in the blanks provided.

1. You find classes for working with streams and backing stores in the _____ namespace.

2. The _____ format is a hierarchical data representation format.

3. The _____ method of the `Console` class reads the next character or function key pressed by the user.

4. Files in the _____ format can allow you to store text, images, and video data.

5. Some objects open unmanaged operating resources, such as file handles. When you are done working with these objects, be sure to call the _____ method to release the unmanaged resources back to the operating system.

6. _____ do not have a graphical user interface; they use a text-mode console window to interact with users.

7. _____ describes the structure of an XML document.

8. The _____ are the values passed to the Main method from the operating system.

9. The .NET Framework's classes to work with XML data are stored organized as part of the _____ namespace.

10. _____ describes the rules by which each character is represented inside a text file.

Multiple Choice

Circle the letter that corresponds to the best answer.

1. Your application needs to store the product image out to a disk file. You'd like to minimize the size of the disk file. Which object should you use to write the file?
   a. FileStream
   b. StreamWriter
   c. BinaryWriter
   d. XmlWriter

2. You are developing a Console Application by using C#. When the user presses a key, your program needs to respond immediately. Which of the following methods of the Console class should you use?
   a. Read
   b. ReadKey
   c. ReadLine
   d. OpenStandardInput

3. You are developing a C# application that creates text files. You write the following code:

   ```
   using (StreamWriter sw =
       new StreamWriter("file.txt"))
   {
       sw.Write("Sample Text");
   }
   ```

   When the text is written to the file, what encoding scheme is used?
   a. UTF8Encoding
   b. UTF7Encoding
   c. ASCIIEncoding
   d. UnicodeEncoding

4. You are developing an application that manipulates XML data. You are reviewing the rules that make XML data well-formed and valid. Which of the following statements are true? (Choose all that apply)
   a. Any XML that conforms to the syntactical rules for XML is considered well-formed.
   b. Any XML that conforms to the syntactical rules for XML is considered valid.
   c. When an XML file conforms to a predefined schema, the file is considered to be well-formed.
   d. When an XML file conforms to a predefined schema, the file is considered to be valid.
   e. XML schema must be present in the same file as the XML data.

5. You are writing a C# program that writes data to a binary file. You write the following code:

   ```
   static void WriteBinaryFile(string fileName)
   {
       Int32 int32Data = 5;
       string stringData = "Sample String";
       Single singleData = 3.141f;
       bool boolData = true;

       using (BinaryWriter writer =
           new BinaryWriter(
           File.Open(fileName, FileMode.Create)))
   ```

```
        {
            writer.Write(int32Data);
            writer.Write(stringData);
            writer.Write(singleData);
            writer.Write(boolData);
        }
    }
```

You now need to read data from this file. Which of the following code segments should you choose?

a.

```
static void ReadBinaryFile(string fileName)
{
    if (File.Exists(fileName))
    {
        using (BinaryReader reader =
            new BinaryReader(
            File.Open(fileName, FileMode.Open)))
        {
            Console.WriteLine(reader.ReadInt32());
            Console.WriteLine(reader.ReadString());
            Console.WriteLine(reader.ReadSingle());
            Console.WriteLine(reader.ReadBoolean());
        }
    }
}
```

b.

```
static void ReadBinaryFile(string fileName)
{
    if (File.Exists(fileName))
    {
        using (BinaryReader reader =
            new BinaryReader(
            File.Open(fileName, FileMode.Open)))
        {
            Console.WriteLine(reader.ReadBoolean());
            Console.WriteLine(reader.ReadSingle());
            Console.WriteLine(reader.ReadString());
            Console.WriteLine(reader.ReadInt32());
        }
    }
}
```

c.

```
static void ReadBinaryFile(string fileName)
{
    if (File.Exists(fileName))
    {
        using (BinaryReader reader =
            new BinaryReader(
            File.Open(fileName, FileMode.Open)))
        {
            Console.WriteLine(reader.ReadString());
            Console.WriteLine(reader.ReadString());
```

```
                    Console.WriteLine(reader.ReadString());
                    Console.WriteLine(reader.ReadString());
                }
            }
        }
```

d.

```
    static void ReadBinaryFile(string fileName)
    {
        if (File.Exists(fileName))
        {
            using (BinaryReader reader =
                new BinaryReader(
                File.Open(fileName, FileMode.Open)))
            {
                Console.WriteLine(reader.ReadBytes());
                Console.WriteLine(reader.ReadBytes ());
                Console.WriteLine(reader.ReadBytes ());
                Console.WriteLine(reader.ReadBytes ());
            }
        }
    }
```

6. Your Windows application needs to perform frequent copy and move operations on a particular file. You want your application to be as optimized as possible. Which of the following classes should you use to perform these operations?
   a. `File`
   b. `FileInfo`
   c. `FileStream`
   d. `Stream`

7. You are developing a C# application that creates text files. You need to use an encoding scheme that supports storing characters from international languages in the text file. Which encoding scheme should you use?
   a. UTF8Encoding
   b. UTF7Encoding
   c. ASCIIEncoding
   d. UnicodeEncoding

8. You are developing a C# application that reads data from disk files. The disk files stores text and video in a pre-defined and structured format. Which of the following .NET Framework class should you use to read such data from disk files?
   a. StreamReader
   b. BinaryReader
   c. XmlReader
   d. StringReader

9. You are developing a C# application that manipulates disk files. The program needs to copy, delete and move the disk files. Which of the following .NET Framework class should you use to manipulate disk files?
   a. File
   b. Directory
   c. FileStream
   d. MemoryStream

10. You are developing a C# application that process data in XML files. You are analyzing an XML document with the following data:

```xml
<?xml version="1.0" encoding="utf-8"?>
<!--Customer List-->
<Customers>
    <Customer Id="ALFKI">
        <CompanyName>Alfreds Futterkiste</CompanyName>
        <Phone>030-0074321</Phone>
    </Customer>
    <Customer Id="EASTC">
        <CompanyName>Eastern Connection</CompanyName>
        <Phone>(171) 555-0297</Phone>
    </Customers>
</Customer>
```

Which of the following observations are true for this XML document? (Select all that apply)
a. The XML document is well formed
b. The XML document is not well formed
c. The XML document is valid
d. The XML document is not valid

Competency Assessment

Project 5-1: Working with Encoding

You are developing a program that manipulates text files. You need to develop a console application that writes a text file by using the Unicode encoding scheme. You also need to read the text from the file that was created. How would you write such a program?

Project 5-2: Working with Typed XML Data

You are developing a program that reads and writes XML data. Your program should be able to read and write typed values rather than their string representation. How would you write such a program?

Proficiency Assessment

Project 5-3: Working with Console Input

You are developing a program that manipulates text input from the console. You need to develop a console application that accepts text from users and converts that text to uppercase letters. The application should not convert input that is not characters, but it should still output this input. How would you write such a program?

Project 5-4: Append to a Text File

You are developing a program that manipulates text files. Your program needs to open the LogFile.txt file (or create the file if it does not already exist) and then append a message with the current time to the file. You also need to write the contents of the file to the console window for display. How would you write such a program?

6 LESSON | Understanding Security

EXAM OBJECTIVE MATRIX

SKILLS/CONCEPTS	MTA EXAM OBJECTIVE	MTA EXAM OBJECTIVE NUMBER
Understanding the System.Security Namespace		
Understanding Authentication and Authorization	Understand authentication and authorization.	5.2
Understanding Cryptography	Understand the System Security namespace.	5.1
Understanding Code Access Security	Understand authentication and authorization.	5.2

KEY TERMS

authentication

authorization

code access security

cryptography

permissions

permission sets

public-key encryption

secret-key encryption

Transparency Level 2

You are a software developer for the Northwind Corporation. As part of your work, you need to plan and configure security for the applications that you develop. In some cases, this involves computer security–keeping untrusted applications from harming the operating system or the user's critical data files. In other situations, this involves user security–controlling who can use a particular application.

■ Understanding the System.Security Namespace

↓ THE BOTTOM LINE

The System.Security namespace contains classes that represent the .NET Framework security system. The namespace provides classes for authentication, access control, and for cryptography service among other things.

The .NET Framework provides several classes that help developers write secure code and control access to protected resources. This lesson also introduces you to role-based security and code-access security. Role-based security is concerned with authorizing user access to application-managed resources and operations while the Code access security is concerned with controlling what operations a piece of code can perform or not perform.

The chapter also discusses .NET Framework's implementation of standard cryptography algorithms. These algorithms help you to encrypt and decrypt the information and make sure that message integrity is preserved.

■ Understanding Authentication and Authorization

↓ THE BOTTOM LINE

Authentication refers to the process of obtaining credentials from a user and verifying his or her identity. After an identity has been authenticated, it can be authorized to use various resources. ***Authorization*** refers to granting rights based on that identity.

Authentication and authorization are closely intertwined and often work together. Applications will first use authentication to verify the user's identity and then use the identity information to determine the actions that a user is authorized to perform. This section discusses the process of authentication and authorization in detail.

Using Authentication

Authentication refers to the process of obtaining credentials from a user and verifying his or her identity.

CERTIFICATION READY
How does authentication work in the .NET Framework?
5.2

The process of authentication validates the user's credentials against some authority. One common authentication authority is provided by Windows. When you log in to Windows, your Windows identity is available to the .NET applications to use in making security decisions. Those decisions are handled by the .NET Framework role-based security scheme. Many other authentication mechanisms exist, such as basic, digest, Passport, form-based and custom-defined.

Role-based security revolves around two interfaces: `IIdentity` and `IPrincipal`. For applications that use Windows accounts in role-based security, these interfaces are implemented by the `WindowsIdentity` and `WindowsPrincipal` objects, respectively.

The `WindowsIdentity` object represents the Windows user who is running the current code. The properties of this object allow you to retrieve information such as the username and his authentication method.

The `WindowsPrincipal` object adds functionality to the `WindowsIdentity` object. The `WindowsPrincipal` object represents the entire security context of the user who is running the current code, including any roles to which he belongs. When the CLR (Common Language Runtime) decides which role-based permissions to assign to your code, it inspects the `WindowsPrincipal` object.

The following exercise shows you how to use the `WindowsIdentity` object to find authentication information for a user.

→ USE AUTHENTICATION

GET READY. To use authentication, perform the following steps:

1. Create a new project based on the Console Application template. Name the project as GetWindowsIdentity. Name the project's solution as Lesson06.

2. In the Program class, add the following using directive:

   ```
   using System.Security.Principal;
   ```

3. Modify the code inside the Main method as follows:

   ```
   static void Main(string[] args)
   {
       AppDomain.CurrentDomain.SetPrincipalPolicy(
           PrincipalPolicy.WindowsPrincipal);
   // Once the Principal Policy is set to
   // WindowsPrincipal the WindowsIdentity is available
       WindowsIdentity identity =
           WindowsIdentity.GetCurrent();
       Console.WriteLine("Windows Principal: {0}",
           identity.Name);
       Console.WriteLine("Authentication Type: {0}",
           identity.AuthenticationType);
       Console.WriteLine("Is Authenticated? {0}",
           identity.IsAuthenticated);
       Console.WriteLine("Is Anonymous? {0}",
           identity.IsAnonymous);
       Console.WriteLine("Is Guest? {0}",
           identity.IsGuest);
       Console.WriteLine("Is System? {0}",
           identity.IsSystem);
   }
   ```

4. Click **Project > Set as StartUp Project** to set the project as the startup project.

5. Build and run the program (press **Ctrl+F5**) and review the messages in the console window (see Figure 6-1).

Figure 6-1

Using authentication

The code in this exercise first uses the SetPrincipalPolicy method to tell the CLR that the WindowsPrincipal principal policy is in use. Next, the program gets the current windows identity and accesses several properties associated with it, including whether the user is authenticated or not.

TAKE NOTE *

You must set the current application domain's principal policy to the enumeration value `WindowsPrincipal`. By default, the principal policy is set to `UnauthenticatedPrincipal`. If you do not set the principal policy to `WindowsPrincipal`, the `WindowsIdentity.GetCurrent` method will fail.

Using Authorization

Authorization is the process of determining whether an authenticated identity is allowed to perform a requested action.

CERTIFICATION READY
How does authorization work in the .NET Framework?
5.2

You can use .NET Framework role-based security to implement authorization. One way to manage role-based security is to use the `IsInRole` method of the `WindowsPrincipal` object. This method can be used to determine whether the current user is in a specific windows group. The result of this method call can be used to modify your application's user interface or to perform other tasks.

There are three available overloaded forms of the `IsInRole` method:

- `IsInRole(WindowsBuiltInRole)`: This form uses one of the `WindowsBuiltInRole` enumerations to check for membership in the standard Windows groups.
- `IsInRole(string)`: This form checks for membership in a group with the specified name.
- `IsInRole(integer)`: This form checks for membership in a group by using the specified role identifier (RID). RIDs are assigned by the operating system and provide a language-independent way to identify groups.

The following exercise demonstrates the use of the `IsInRole` method to authorize a user.

⊕ USE AUTHORIZATION

GET READY. To use authorization, perform the following steps:

1. Create a new project based on the Console Application template. Name the project as UsingAuthorization.

2. In the Program class, add the following `using` directive:

```
using System.Security.Principal;
using System.Threading;
```

3. In the Program.cs file, modify the code inside the Program class as follows:

```
static void Main(string[] args)
{
    AppDomain.CurrentDomain.SetPrincipalPolicy(
        PrincipalPolicy.WindowsPrincipal);
// The WindowsPrincipal is available from
// the Thread class
    WindowsPrincipal principal =
        (WindowsPrincipal) Thread.CurrentPrincipal;
    bool isAdmin = principal.IsInRole(
        WindowsBuiltInRole.Administrator);

    Console.WriteLine(
        "You are {0}in the Administrators role",
        isAdmin ? "" : "not ");
}
```

4. Set the project as the startup project.

5. Build and run the program (press **Ctrl+F5**) and then review the output in the console window.

The output of this program displays a message indicating whether the logged on user is a member of the built-in administrator role.

There are times when the focus of authorization is more about requiring membership in a particular role before a task can be allowed. To help with these cases, there is an alternative way to manage authorization by performing security checking with the `PrincipalPermission` class. The `PrincipalPermission.Demand` method checks at runtime if the current security principal matches the one specified by current permission. If the current principal does not pass the security check, a `SecurityException` is raised. If no `SecurityException` is thrown, the demand for the security permission succeeds.

The following exercise shows you how to use the `PrincipalPermission` class to implement authorization.

→ USE THE PRINCIPALPERMISSION CLASS TO IMPLEMENT AUTHORIZATION

GET READY. To use the `PrincipalPermission` class to implement authorization, perform the following steps:

1. Create a new project based on the Console Application template. Name the project as UsingPrincipalPermission.

2. In the Program.cs file, add the code for the following using directive:

```
using System.Security.Principal;
using System.Security.Permissions;
```

3. Modify the code inside the `Program` class as follows:

```
static void Main(string[] args)
{
    AppDomain.CurrentDomain.SetPrincipalPolicy(
        PrincipalPolicy.WindowsPrincipal);

    string roleName = "BUILTIN\\Administrators";

    PrincipalPermission pp = new
        PrincipalPermission(null, roleName);
    try
    {
        pp.Demand();
        Console.WriteLine(
            "You are in the {0} role",
            roleName);
    }
    catch (Exception ex)
    {
        Console.WriteLine("Exception: {0}",
            ex.Message);
    }
}
```

4. Set the project as the startup project.

5. Build and run the program (press **Ctrl+F5**) and then review the output in the console window.

The output of this program displays a message indicating whether the logged on user is a member of the built-in administrator role.

■ Understanding Cryptography

The System.Security.Cryptography namespace contains various classes that provide cryptography services, including encryption and decryption of data, hashing, random number generation, and message authentication.

Non-secure networks such as the Internet do not inherently provide a way of secure communication between the sender and the receiver. When you send information over such networks, it is possible that a third-party can eavesdrop and view the data and, even worse, possibly modify the data. In addition, there is no way to verify the sender and receiver of the message.

Cryptography provides a way to overcome these problems. *Cryptography* encrypts the data so that it cannot be by viewed by unauthorized users and to detect whether the data has been modified. Cryptography also helps establish the identity of the sender so that you can trust that the message is actually coming from the claimed sender.

Understanding Encryption and Decryption

One of the major goals of cryptography is to protect data by encrypting it. Encrypted data can be decrypted only by someone with a key.

The .NET Framework provides two different types of encryption algorithms:

- Secret-key encryption
- Public-key encryption

Using Secret-Key Encryption

In the *secret-key encryption* technique, both the sender and receiver of the message share a secret encryption key. The sender encrypts the message before sending it across, and the receiver uses the same key to decrypt the message.

In secret-key encryption, the secret key must be protected from unauthorized use. Anyone with the access to the secret key can not only decrypt the messages but can also encrypt the messages while claiming that they came from the original sender.

This encryption is also known as symmetric encryption because the same key is used for both encryption and decryption.

The .NET Framework provides the following classes to implement the secret key algorithms:

- `AesManaged`
- `DESCryptoServiceProvider`
- `HMACSHA1`
- `RC2CryptoServiceProvider`
- `RijndaelManaged`
- `TripleDESCryptoServiceProvider`

AesManaged and RijndaelManaged provide highest-level of encryption. The AesManaged class implements the Advanced Encryption Standard (AES) symmetric algorithm. The classes with the suffix "Provider" provide a cryptographic service provider (CSP) implementation of their corresponding algorithm and also provide useful services such as encrypt and decrypt.

TAKE NOTE*

The AesManaged class functions the same way as the RijndaelManaged class but limits blocks to 128 bits. The AES algorithm is compliant with the Federal Information Processing Standards (FIPS) whereas the Rijndael algorithm is not.

If you use the same secret key for encryption, an attacker can study encrypted data to possibly find patterns and attempt to decrypt the data. To mitigate this risk, the symmetric encryption algorithms also use a random Initialization Vector (IV) for encryption. Attaching a random IV with your data makes it difficult for an attacker to recognize patterns in encryption.

Let's try to understand how this works with a very simple example. Let's encrypt "New York" using an IV that is one character long. Let's also say that you randomly select the IV to be "z". Now the data that you will effectively encrypt using a secret key is "zNewYork". Let's say that the encrypted data is "jyhsu487$^$". When it comes time for decryption, you decrypt the encrypted data using the secret key, yielding "zNewYork" and then you take out the IV from the data yielding you with the original data, "New York". Next time, when you encrypt, you may want to use the same secret key but a different random IV.

The following exercise demonstrates how to use the AesManaged class to encrypt and decrypt data.

➔ USE SECRET-KEY ENCRYPTION

GET READY. To use the AesManaged class to encrypt and decrypt data, perform the following steps:

1. Create a new project based on the Console Application template. Name the project as SecretKeyEncryption.

2. In the Program.cs file, add the following using directives:

```
using System.IO;
using System.Security.Cryptography;
```

3. In the Program.cs file, modify the code inside the Program class as follows:

```
static void Main(string[] args)
{
    string plainText =
        "Lorem ipsum dolor sit amet...";
// Create AesManaged to generate the key
// and initial vector values
    using (AesManaged aes =
        new AesManaged())
    {
        Console.WriteLine(
            "Before Encryption: {0}", plainText);
        byte[] encryptedBytes =
            AesEncrypt(plainText, aes.Key, aes.IV);
        string decryptedText =
            AesDecrypt(encryptedBytes,
            aes.Key, aes.IV);
        Console.WriteLine(
            "After Decryption : {0}", decryptedText);
    }
}
```

```csharp
        private static byte[] AesEncrypt(
            string plainText, byte[] key, byte[] iv)
        {
            byte[] encryptedBytes;
// Create another AesManaged object, but
// set the key and initial vector values
// to those passed as parameters
            using (AesManaged aes = new AesManaged())
            {
                aes.Key = key;
                aes.IV = iv;

                ICryptoTransform encryptor =
                    aes.CreateEncryptor(aes.Key, aes.IV);
                using (MemoryStream ms = new MemoryStream())
                {
                    using (CryptoStream cs =
                        new CryptoStream(ms, encryptor,
                            CryptoStreamMode.Write))
                    {

                        using (StreamWriter sw =
                            new StreamWriter(cs))
                        {
                            sw.Write(plainText);
                        }
                        encryptedBytes = ms.ToArray();
                    }
                }
            }
            return encryptedBytes;
        }

        private static string AesDecrypt(
            byte[] encryptedBytes, byte[] key, byte[] iv)
        {
            string decryptedText = null;
// Create another AesManaged object, but
// set the key and initial vector values
// to those passed as parameters
            using (AesManaged aes = new AesManaged())
            {
                aes.Key = key;
                aes.IV = iv;

                ICryptoTransform decryptor =
                    aes.CreateDecryptor(aes.Key, aes.IV);
                using (MemoryStream ms =
                    new MemoryStream(encryptedBytes))
                {
                    using (CryptoStream cs =
                        new CryptoStream(ms, decryptor,
                            CryptoStreamMode.Read))
                    {
                        using (StreamReader sr =
                            new StreamReader(cs))
```

```
                    {
                        decryptedText = sr.ReadToEnd();
                    }
                }
            }
        }
        return decryptedText;
    }
```

4. Set the project as the startup project.

5. Build and run the program (press **Ctrl+F5**), and then review the output in the console window.

In this exercise, you first create an instance of the *AesManaged* class. The secret key and the IV are specified by using the *Key* and the *IV* properties, respectively. You can provide your own key and IV, or else you can use the key and IV randomly generated for you by the AesManaged class, as in the exercise. The program then encrypts the given data as part of the `AesEncrypt` method and then decrypts the encrypted data as part of the `AesDecrypt` method.

The `AesEncrypt` method uses the `AesManaged.CreateEncryptor` to create an encryptor using the secret key and initial vector values, which is used by the `CryptoStream` object to write the encrypted data.

The `AesDecrypt` method works in the opposite direction; it uses the `AesManaged.CreateDecryptor` to create a decryptor using the same shared secret key and initial vector values, which is used by the `CryptoStream` object to read the decrypted data.

Using Public-Key Encryption

> *Public-key encryption* protects data by using a set of two cryptographically paired keys. One key is called a private key, and it is known only to its owner. The second key is called a public key, which belongs to the owner, but as the name suggests, it can be made public to anyone.

The public key and the private key are cryptographically paired. That is, the data encrypted using a public key can only be decrypted using the corresponding private key. Additionally, the data signed by a private key can be verified only by the corresponding public key.

Let's say Bob wants to transfer an encrypted message to Alice. Bob and Alice can use the public key encryption as follows:

- Alice generates a private/public key pair. She keeps the private key secret and sends her public key to Bob in an email.
- Bob takes Alice's public key and encrypts the message using it. Bob then sends the encrypted message to Alice.
- Alice receives the encrypted message and uses her private key to decrypt the message.

If Alice were to transfer an encrypted message to Bob, the entire process would be done in reverse. She would then use Bob's public key for encryption and Bob would use his private key to decrypt that message. When a sender and receiver communicate encrypted data by using the public key cryptography, they don't need to share the private-key information. Only the public key is shared.

Because the private key is known only to the owner of the key, it can be used for providing digital signatures. Sending an authenticated message between Alice and Bob will work as follows:

- Alice signs the message using her private key and sends the message to Bob along with her public key.

- Bob receives the message and uses Alice's public key to verify that the message is indeed sent by Alice and has not been tampered with during the transfer.

The .NET Framework provides the following classes to implement the public-key encryption algorithms:

- DSACryptoServiceProvider
- RSACryptoServiceProvider
- ECDiffieHellmanCng
- ECDsaCng

In general, the public-key algorithms are more limited in their uses than secret-key algorithms. The RSACryptoServiceProvider class implements the RSA algorithm and allows both encryption and signing. The DSACryptoServiceProvider class implements the DSA algorithm and can be used only for signing. The ECDiffieHellmanCng class implements the Diffie-Hellman algorithm and can be used only for key generation. The ECDsaCng class provides an implementation of the Elliptic Curve Digital Signature Algorithm (ECDSA). This class internally uses the new cryptography API called Cryptography API: Next Generation, which was introduced with Windows Vista.

The following exercise shows you how to use the RSACryptoServiceProvider class to encrypt and decrypt messages.

 USE PUBLIC-KEY ENCRYPTION

GET READY. To use the RSACryptoServiceProvider class to encrypt and decrypt messages, perform the following steps:

1. Create a new project based on the Console Application template. Name the project as PublicKeyEncryption.

2. In the Program.cs file, make sure that you have the following using directives:

```
using System.Text;
using System.Security.Cryptography;
```

3. Modify the code inside the Program class as follows:

```
static void Main(string[] args)
{
    UnicodeEncoding encoding = new UnicodeEncoding();
    Byte[] plainText = encoding.GetBytes(
            "Lorem ipsum dolor sit amet...");
    Byte[] encrypted, decrypted;

    using (var rsa = new RSACryptoServiceProvider())
    {
        Console.WriteLine(
            "Before Encryption: {0}",
            encoding.GetString(plainText));

        encrypted = RSAEncrypt(plainText,
                rsa.ExportParameters(false));
        decrypted = RSADecrypt(encrypted,
                rsa.ExportParameters(true));

        Console.WriteLine(
            "After Decryption : {0}",
                encoding.GetString(decrypted));
```

```
        }
    }

    private static byte[] RSAEncrypt(byte[] plainText,
        RSAParameters rSAParameters)
{
// The encrypted message would be sent by anyone
// with the public key.
    byte[] encrypted;
    using (var rsa = new RSACryptoServiceProvider())
    {
        rsa.ImportParameters(rSAParameters);
        encrypted = rsa.Encrypt(plainText, true);
    }
    return encrypted;
}

    private static byte[] RSADecrypt(byte[] encrypted,
        RSAParameters rSAParameters)
{
// The decrypted message would only be accessible
// to the person holding the private key.
    byte[] decrypted;
    using (var rsa = new RSACryptoServiceProvider())
    {
        rsa.ImportParameters(rSAParameters);
        decrypted = rsa.Decrypt(encrypted, true);
    }
    return decrypted;
}
```

4. Set the project as the startup project.

5. Build and run the program (press **Ctrl+F5**), and then review the output in the console window.

The program uses the public-private key-pair automatically generated by the RSACryptoServiceProvider class when the constructor is called. The program first uses only the public key to encrypt the given text as part of the RSAEncrypt method and then decrypts the encrypted data using the private key as part of the RSADecrypt method. When you use the ExportParameters method with the false argument, only the public key is exported; the private key is not exported. On the other hand, when you call the ExportParameters method with the true value, the private key is exported as well.

The RSAEncrypt method uses the RSACryptoServiceProvider.Encrypt method to encrypt the data. The RSADecrypt method works in the opposite direction and uses the RSACryptoServiceProvider.Decrypt method to decrypt the data.

■ Understanding Code Access Security

↓
THE BOTTOM LINE

Code access security is a security mechanism provided by the .NET Framework to manage what a code running on a computer system is allowed to do. Code access security can protect a computer from getting harmed by running code from the untrusted sources, or it can help prevent trusted code from accidentally compromising security.

CERTIFICATION READY
How does code access security work in the .NET Framework?
5.2

Code access security defines what the code running on a computer system is allowed to do. Code access security offers protections in the following two situations:

- Enforces that the code originating from unknown or untrusted source runs with added protection.
- If you specify the operations your code is allowed to perform, the code access security system can help reduce the chances that your code is misused by malicious code to perform unintended operations.

The .NET Framework 4 simplifies code access security by using the security transparency as the default mechanism for security enforcement. Transparency is a security enforcement mechanism that separates code that can do privileged things (also called critical code), such as calling native code, and code that cannot (also called transparent code). Transparent code can execute commands within the bounds of the permission set it is operating in, but it cannot execute, derive from, or contain critical code. Security transparency existed in earlier versions of .NET Framework but a new Level 2 transparency was introduced in .NET Framework 4. *Transparency Level 2* groups the code in the three categories shown in Table 6-1.

Table 6-1

Level 2 Transparency Categories

CATEGORY	SECURITY ATTRIBUTE	DESCRIPTION
Transparent	`SecurityTransparentAttribute`	The code in this category cannot do anything that is security-sensitive. It cannot call unsafe code or code that is classified as security-critical. Partial-trust code is always transparent.
Security-Critical	`SecurityCriticalAttribute`	This code can do anything. This code cannot be called from code that is classified as Transparent.
Safe-Critical	`SecuritySafeCriticalAttribute`	This code can do anything, but it performs proper security checks and validation before calling security-critical code. This code can be called from the code classified as Transparent.

The following exercise helps you explore code access security settings.

EXPLORE CODE ACCESS SECURITY SETTINGS

GET READY. To explore code access security settings, perform the following steps:

1. Create a new project based on the Console Application template. Name the project as CodeAccessSecurity.

2. In the Program.cs file, add the following using directives:

```
using System.Reflection;
using System.Security;
using System.Security.Policy;
```

3. Modify the code inside the Program class as follows:

```csharp
static void Main(string[] args)
{
    Assembly assembly =
        Assembly.GetExecutingAssembly();

    Console.WriteLine(
        "Assembly SecurityZone: {0}",
        assembly.Evidence
        .GetHostEvidence<Zone>().SecurityZone);
    Console.WriteLine(
        "Assembly SecurityRuleSet: {0}",
        assembly.SecurityRuleSet);
    Console.WriteLine(
        "Assembly IsFullyTusted? {0}",
        assembly.IsFullyTrusted);

    Type type = typeof(Program);
    Console.WriteLine(
        "Class IsSecurityTransparent? {0}",
        type.IsSecurityTransparent);
    Console.WriteLine(
        "Class IsSecuritySafeCritical? {0}",
        type.IsSecuritySafeCritical);
    Console.WriteLine(
        "Class IsSecurityCritical? {0}",
        type.IsSecurityCritical);

    //Call a property with SecurityCriticalAttribute
    try
    {
        var permissionSet = assembly.PermissionSet;
        Console.WriteLine("Calling code with " +
        "SecurityCriticalAttribute succeeded");
    }
    catch (Exception ex)
    {
        Console.WriteLine(
            "Calling code with " +
            "SecurityCriticalAttribute failed: {0}",
            ex.Message);
    }
    Console.WriteLine(
        "Press any key to continue...");
    Console.ReadKey();
}
```

4. Set the project as the startup project.

5. Build and run the program (**press Ctrl+F5**). The program displays output similar to Figure 6-2.

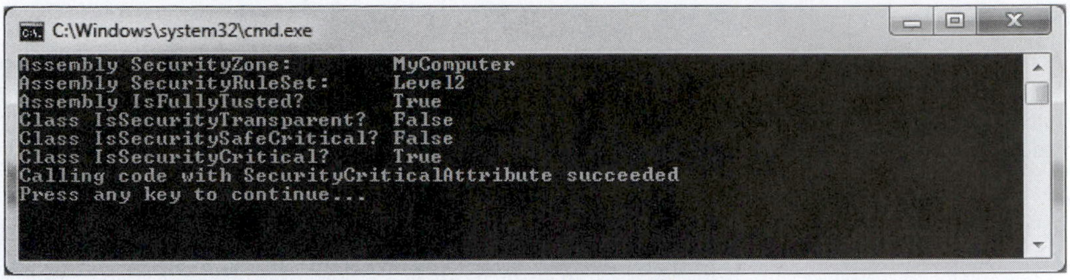

Figure 6-2

Exploring code access security

```
C:\Windows\system32\cmd.exe
Assembly SecurityZone:          MyComputer
Assembly SecurityRuleSet:       Level2
Assembly IsFullyTusted?         True
Class IsSecurityTransparent?    False
Class IsSecuritySafeCritical?   False
Class IsSecurityCritical?       True
Calling code with SecurityCriticalAttribute succeeded
Press any key to continue...
```

As shown in the Figure 6-2, the program displays the following information:

- The assembly evidence specifies where the assembly code originated from. In this exercise, the assembly evidence is part of the MyComputer security zone. This is due to the fact that code originated and is being executed from the local computer.

- The SecurityRuleSet for the assembly is Level2, which is the default level for the .NET Framework 4.0. Other values for the SecurityRuleSet include Level1 and None. You can also explicitly specify this setting by using the SecurityRulesAttribute as follows:

      [assembly: SecurityRules(SecurityRuleSet.Level2)]

- The assembly is fully trusted. The .NET Framework 4.0 security setting assigns FullTrust permissions to any code that runs on the local computer.

- The code is classified as SecurityCritical. That is, there are no restrictions for this code and it can do anything, including calling other security-critical code.

Unlike previous versions of the .NET Framework, even if the Evidence of the assembly is Intranet or Internet, if the code is being executed locally from either the command prompt or Windows Explorer, it is fully trusted and is considered security-critical as shown in Figure 6-3.

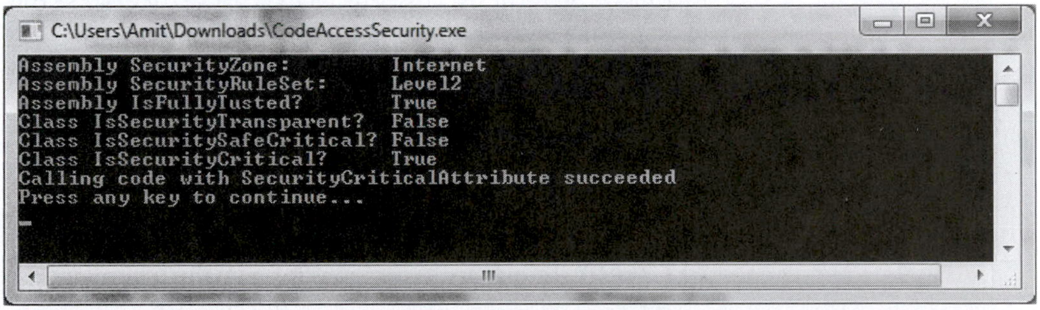

Figure 6-3

Code that executes locally is fully trusted and is SecurityCritical irrespective of the SecurityZone

```
C:\Users\Amit\Downloads\CodeAccessSecurity.exe
Assembly SecurityZone:          Internet
Assembly SecurityRuleSet:       Level2
Assembly IsFullyTusted?         True
Class IsSecurityTransparent?    False
Class IsSecuritySafeCritical?   False
Class IsSecurityCritical?       True
Calling code with SecurityCriticalAttribute succeeded
Press any key to continue...
```

In some cases, an assembly might not need all the permissions to run, and you might want to explicitly reduce the permissions available to the code in order to reduce the risk of accidental or unauthorized use of the permissions. To execute the code in the previous exercise in the SecurityTransparent setting, you need to add the following attribute to the assembly:

      [assembly: SecurityTransparent()]

The SecurityTransparentAttribute class is part of the System.Security namespace. As this attribute is applied to the assembly, you'll need to place this attribute outside the namespace block in the source code. When you run the program after running the attribute, you'll get the output shown in Figure 6-4.

```
C:\Windows\system32\cmd.exe
Assembly SecurityZone:        MyComputer
Assembly SecurityRuleSet:     Level2
Assembly IsFullyTrusted?      True
Class IsSecurityTransparent?  True
Class IsSecuritySafeCritical? False
Class IsSecurityCritical?     False
Calling code with SecurityCriticalAttribute failed: Attempt by security transpar
ent method 'CodeAccessSecurity.Program.Main(System.String[])' to access security
 critical method 'System.Reflection.Assembly.get_PermissionSet()' failed.
Press any key to continue...
```

Here, the code is running as `SecurityTransparentCode` and it cannot call any
`SecurityCriticalCode` such as accessing the `PermissionSet` property of the `assembly`
object, and as a result, the code throws an exception confirming that the code is running with
reduced permissions.

Managing Permissions

Permissions refer to the actions that a code is allowed to or not allowed to perform.
Permission sets are a predefined collection of permissions that are applied together.

The code that runs on the desktop runs in the full trust mode. That is, the code has all
permissions. You can limit what code can or cannot do by running the code inside a security
sandbox. Inside a security sandbox, the code is only allowed to do the actions that are defined
by the permissions given to the sandbox.

The System.Security.Permissions namespace defines the classes that specify the permissions
you can apply to an assembly declaratively or programmatically. There are a large number
of permission classes in this namespace giving you fine-grained control over what you want
to achieve. Some of the classes include the `FileIOPermission` class to control the ability
to access files and folders, the `RegistryPermission` class to control if the code can
manipulate the Windows Registry, the `EnvironmentPermission` class to control access
to the environment variables and so on.

The following exercise shows how to manage permission for partially trusted code.

MANAGE PERMISSIONS FOR PARTIALLY TRUSTED CODE

GET READY. To manage permissions for partially trusted code, perform the following steps:

1. Create a new project based on the Class Library template. Name the project as
   PermissionDemoLibrary.
2. Change the default class file name from Class1.cs to PermissionDemo.cs.
3. Modify the code in the PermissionDemo.cs file as follows:

```csharp
using System;
using System.IO;
using System.Security;

[assembly: AllowPartiallyTrustedCallers()]
namespace PermissionDemoLibrary
{
    [SecuritySafeCritical()]
    public class PermissionDemo : MarshalByRefObject
    {
```

```
public bool WriteFile(string path)
{
    bool canAccess = false;
    try
    {
        using (StreamWriter writer
            = File.CreateText(path))
        {
            writer.WriteLine(
            "Lorem ipsum dolor sit amet...");
            canAccess = true;
        }
    }
    catch (SecurityException)
    {
        canAccess = false;
    }
    return canAccess;
    }
  }
}
```

4. Build the PermissionDemoLibrary project and verify that there are no error messages.

5. Add a new project based on the Console Application template. Name the project as PermissionsDemoApplication.

6. Click **Project > Add Reference**.

7. Select the **Projects** tab, click **PermissionDemoLibrary**, and then click **OK**.

8. Modify the code in the Program class with the following code:

```
using System;
using System.IO;
using System.Reflection;
using System.Security;
using System.Security.Permissions;
using PermissionDemoLibrary;

namespace PermissionDemoApplication
{
    class Program
    {
        static void Main(string[] args)
        {
            string fileName = "TestFile.txt";
            string path = Path.GetDirectoryName(
                Assembly.GetExecutingAssembly()
                .Location) + fileName;

            var permSet = new
                PermissionSet(PermissionState.None);
            permSet.AddPermission(
                new SecurityPermission(
                    SecurityPermissionFlag.Execution));
            //permSet.AddPermission(
            // new FileIOPermission(
            // FileIOPermissionAccess.AllAccess,
            // path));
```

```
var adSetup = AppDomain.CurrentDomain
    .SetupInformation;
var appDomain =
    AppDomain.CreateDomain("SandBox",
    AppDomain.CurrentDomain.Evidence,
    adSetup, permSet);
var handle =
    appDomain.CreateInstance(
    "PermissionDemoLibrary",
"PermissionDemoLibrary.PermissionDemo");
var pd = handle.Unwrap() as
    PermissionDemo;

Console.WriteLine("Can access {0}? {1}",
    fileName, pd.WriteFile(path));
Console.WriteLine(
    "Press any key to continue...");
Console.ReadKey();
        }
    }
}
```

9. Build and run the PermissionDemoApplication project. The console window displays a message indicating that it can't access TestFile.txt.

10. Uncomment the following lines of code in the `Program` class:

    ```
    permSet.AddPermission(new FileIOPermission(
    FileIOPermissionAccess.AllAccess, path));
    ```

11. Build and run the PermissionDemoApplication project again. You will see that the console window displays a message saying that it can access TestFile.txt. Look for the TestFile.txt in project's output folder and check the contents of the file.

In this exercise, the PermissionDemoApplication creates a security sandbox by using the `AppDomain.CreateDomain` method. Next, it adds the `PermissionDemoLibrary` assembly to the sandbox and assigns permissions to the sandbox. In this case, the code in the `PermissionDemoLibrary` is considered to be hosted code and is security transparent and is considered partially trusted.

The `PermissionDemoLibrary` assembly is marked with the `AllowPartiallyTrustedCallers` attribute. This attribute allows the assembly to be called by partially trusted code such as our sandbox. The `PermissionDemo` class is marked with the `SecuritySafeCritical` attribute so that it can be called from the security-transparent code. Additionally, this means that `PermissionDemoLibrary` assembly performs security checks before calling the security-critical code.

When you run the code for the first time, the sandbox does not have permission to perform file input and output and, therefore, the code in the sandbox cannot access the text file. However, before you run the code again, you add file I/O permissions to the sandbox resulting in the file access operation to succeed.

Working with Access Control

Access control refers to security features that control who can access resources such as files or directories in the operating system. Applications call access control functions to set who can access specific resources or control access to resources provided by the application.

There are two basic parts of the access control model:

- Access tokens: when a user logs on, the system authenticates the user's account name and password. If the logon is successful, the system creates an access token. Every process executed on behalf of this user will have a copy of this access token. The access token contains security identifiers that identify the user's account and any group accounts to which the user belongs. The token also contains a list of the privileges held by the user or the user's groups. The system uses this information to identify the user when a process tries to access a securable object or perform a task that requires privileges.

- Security descriptors: a security descriptor identifies the object's owner and the object's access control list (ACL). The ACL contain information about the users allowed or denied access to the object.

The FileStream, Directory, and File classes provide a GetAccessControl method that returns a value of the type FileSecurity.

```
var stream = File.Open(
    "TestFile.txt", FileMode.Open);
var fileSecurity =  stream.GetAccessControl();
```

The FileSecurity object can be used to retrieve the access control list for the specified resource. The GetAccessRules method of the FileSecurity class gets a collection of the access rules associated with the specified security identifier.

```
fileSecurity.GetAccessRules( true, true, typeof(NTAccount))
```

The GetAccessRules method takes three parameters. The first parameter specifies whether to include the access rules explicitly set for the object. The second parameter specifies whether to include inherited access rules, and the third parameter specifies whether the type of the whether the security identifier for which to retrieve access rules is of type SecurityIdentifier or the type NTAccount. The type NTAccount as specified in the previous line of code represents a user or group account.

The return value of GetAccessRules method is a collection of access rules such as the FileSystemAccessRule. The FileSystemAccessRule defines the access rules for a file or directory. Following are some of the properties of the FileSystemAccess class that you can use to determine who has what rights on a file or directory:

- AccessControlType: Specifies whether access is allowed or denied.
- IdentityReference: Identity of the user to which the access rule apply.
- FileSystemRights: Specifies the access rights associated with the rule.

The following code shows how to iterate over the access rule collection and display the access right for a given file:

```
foreach (var item in
    fileSecurity.GetAccessRules(
    true, true, typeof(NTAccount)))
{
    var rule = item as
        FileSystemAccessRule;
    Console.WriteLine(
        "Identity Reference : {0}",
        rule.IdentityReference.Value); ();
    Console.WriteLine(
        "Access Control Type: {0}",
        rule.AccessControlType); ();
    Console.WriteLine(
        "File System Rights : {0}\n",
        rule.FileSystemRights); ();
}
```

SKILL SUMMARY

IN THIS LESSON YOU LEARNED:

- The System.Security namespace contains classes that represent the .NET Framework security system. The namespace provides classes for authentication, access control, and for cryptography service among other things.
- Authentication refers to the process of obtaining credentials from a user and verifying his or her identity. After an identity has been authenticated, it can be authorized to use various resources. Authorization refers to granting rights based on that identity.
- The System.Security.Cryptography namespace provide various classes that provide cryptography services, including encryption and decryption of data, hashing, random number generation, and message authentication.
- In the secret-key encryption technique, both sender and receiver of the message share a secret encryption key. The sender encrypts the message before sending it across and the receiver uses the same key to decrypt the message.
- Public-key encryption uses a set of two keys: a public key and a private key. The data encrypted using a public key can only be decrypted using the corresponding private key. Additionally, the data signed by a private key can be verified only by the corresponding public key.
- Code access security is a security mechanism provided by the .NET Framework to manage what a code running on a computer system is allowed to do. Code access security can protect a computer from getting harmed by running code from the untrusted sources or to help prevent trusted code from accidentally compromising security.

■ Knowledge Assessment

Fill in the Blank

Complete the following sentences by writing the correct word or words in the blanks provided.

1. _____ refers to the process of obtaining credentials from a user and verifying his or her identity.

2. _____ is the process of determining whether an authenticated identity is allowed to perform a requested action.

3. The _____ encryption technique uses a set of two distinct keys that are cryptographically paired.

4. The code classified as _____ cannot do anything that is security-sensitive. This code cannot call any unsafe code or any code that is classified as security-critical.

5. Role-based security revolves around two interfaces: _____ and _____.

6. The _____ method of the WindowsPrincipal object can be used to determine whether the current user is in a specific windows group.

7. The secret-key encryption is also known as _____ encryption because the same key is used for both encryption and decryption.

8. The _____ class implements a public-key cryptography algorithm based on the RSA algorithm and allows both encryption and signing.

9. _____ refer to the actions that code is allowed to or not allowed to perform.

10. The _____ namespace defines the classes that specify the permissions you can apply to an assembly declaratively or programmatically.

Multiple Choice

Circle the letter that corresponds to the best answer.

1. Your application requires the user to be in the Domain Admins group in order to activate certain functions. Which .NET security feature should you use to ensure that the user is in this group?
   a. Code access security
   b. Role-based security
   c. Encryption
   d. Type safety

2. You are developing a program that implements role-based security. You need to check a user for membership in the Windows groups. Which of the following methods should you use to accomplish your requirements?
   a. `WindowsPrincipal.IsInRole` method
   b. `WindowsIdentity.GetCurrent` method
   c. `WindowsIdentity.Impersonate` method
   d. `PrincipalPermission.IsSubsetOf` method

3. You are developing a program that implements role-based security. You need to determine whether the user belongs to a custom Windows user group that has a specified name. Which form of the `WindowsPrincipal.IsInRole` method should you use?
   a. `IsInRole(Int32)`
   b. `IsInRole(SecurityIdentifier)`
   c. `IsInRole(string)`
   d. `IsInRole(WindowsBuiltInRole)`

4. You are developing a C# application that needs to use secret-key encryption. You need to provide the highest-level of encryption that is compliant with the US Federal Information Processing Standards (FIPS). Which cryptography class should you use?
   a. `RijndaelManaged`
   b. `AesManaged`
   c. `TripleDESCryptoServiceProvider`
   d. `DSACryptoServiceProvider`

5. You are developing a C# application that needs to use public-key encryption and digital signing. You need to use an algorithm that provide highest-level of encryption and allow both encryption and signing. Which cryptography class should you use?
   a. `AesManaged`
   b. `RSACryptoServiceProvider`
   c. `DSACryptoServiceProvider`
   d. `TripleDESCryptoServiceProvider`

6. You are developing a C# application that uses the `RSACryptoServiceProvider` class. You need to provide the public key information but protect the private key. What should you do to accomplish this requirement?
   a. Call the `ExportParameters` method with a parameter value of `false`.
   b. Call the `ExportParameters` method with a parameter value of `true`.
   c. Call the `Encrypt` method with a parameter value of `true`.
   d. Call the `Encrypt` method with a parameter value of `false`.

7. You are developing a C# application that uses a variable named asm of the type Assembly. You check that the value of the expression, `asm.IsFullyTrusted` is false. Which of the following statements are true for the assembly? (Choose all that apply)
   a. The assembly is fully trusted
   b. The assembly is partially trusted

   c. All the types in the assembly are running as `SecurityTransparent` code

   d. All the types in the assembly are running as `SecuritySafeCritical` code

   e. All the types in the assembly are running as `SecurityCritical` code

8. You downloaded a .NET assembly from an Internet Website to your local computer. You run the code directly on the local computer. Which of the following statements are true for the assembly? (Choose all that apply)

   a. The assembly is fully trusted

   b. The assembly is partially trusted

   c. All the types in the assembly are running as `SecurityTransparent` code

   d. All the types in the assembly are running as `SecuritySafeCritical` code

   e. All the types in the assembly are running as `SecurityCritical` code

9. You are developing an application that doesn't need to access protected resource. You want to ensure that your code is never used to accidentally or maliciously accesses protected resources. What should you do to accomplish this?

   a. Apply the following attribute to the assembly

```
[assembly: SecurityTransparent()]
```

   b. Apply the following attribute to the assembly

```
[assembly: SecurityCritical()]
```

   c. Apply the following attribute to the assembly

```
[assembly: SecuritySafeCritical()]
```

   d. Apply the following attribute to the assembly

```
[assembly: SecurityRules(SecurityRuleSet.Level2)]
```

10. You need to create a partially trusted host for an assembly in your application. What should you do to accomplish this?

   a. Apply the following attribute to the assembly

```
[assembly: SecurityRules(SecurityRuleSet.Level1)]
```

   b. Apply the following attribute to the assembly

```
[assembly: SecurityRules(SecurityRuleSet.Level2)]
```

   c. Apply the following attribute to the assembly

```
[assembly: AllowPartiallyTrustedCallers()]
```

   d. Use the `AppDomain.CreateDomain` method

■ Competency Assessment

Project 6-1: Using the RijndaelManaged Class for Secret-Key Encryption

You are developing a program that manipulates text files. You need to encrypt and decrypt your files by using the `RijndaelManaged` class. How would you write such a program?

Project 6-2: Getting User Identity and Group Membership

You are developing a program that needs to find out the identity of the logged-in Windows user and the name of the Windows Groups that the user is a member of. How would you write a program to retrieve this information?

Proficiency Assessment

Project 6-3: Working with Access Control List

You are developing a program that manipulates files. You need to find the access control list for a given file such as the access control type and file system rights for the Windows users or group accounts. How would you write such a program?

Project 6-4: Verifying Role Membership

You are developing a program that needs to find out if the logged-in Windows user is a member of the Windows built-in Administrator role. How would you write a program to display this information?

Appendix A
Exam 98-372 Microsoft .NET Fundamentals

Exam Objective	Skill Number	Lesson Number
Understanding .NET Framework Concepts		
Understand basic application settings.	1.1	3
Understand events and event handling in the .NET Framework.	1.2	3
Understand structured exception handling in the .NET Framework.	1.3	3
Understanding Namespaces and Classes in the .NET Framework		
Understand .NET class hierarchies.	2.1	1
Understand Object Oriented Concepts in the .NET Framework.	2.2	1
Understand .NET namespaces.	2.3	1
Understand and create class libraries.	2.4	1
Understand and use different data types in the .NET Framework.	2.5	2
Understand generics.	2.6	2
Understanding .NET Code Compilation		
Understand the fundamentals of Microsoft Intermediate Language (MSIL) and Common Language Infrastructure (CLI).	3.1	4
Understand the use of strong naming.	3.2	4
Understand version control.	3.3	4
Understand assemblies and metadata.	3.4	4
Understanding I/O Classes in the .NET Framework		
Understand .NET file classes.	4.1	5
Understand console I/O.	4.2	5
Understand XML classes in the .NET Framework.	4.3	5
Understanding Security		
Understand the System Security namespace.	5.1	6
Understand authentication and authorization.	5.2	6